THE IMAGE MAKER

TRANSFORMING YOUR LIFE FROM THE INSIDE OUT

AVIS COLE ATTAWAY, LMFT

BALBOA.
PRESS
A DIVISION OF HAY HOUSE

Balboa Press books may be ordered through booksellers or by contacting:

Balboa Press
A Division of Hay House
1663 Liberty Drive
Bloomington, IN 47403
www.balboapress.com
1 (877) 407-4847

Print information available on the last page.

ISBN: 978-1-4525-6620-7 (sc)
ISBN: 978-1-4525-6622-1 (hc)
ISBN: 978-1-4525-6621-4 (e)

Library of Congress Control Number: 2012924129

Balboa Press rev. date: 06/27/2018

To each and every one of my clients, past and present ...
Thank you for all you have taught me.

One discovers that destiny can be diverted,
that one does not need to remain in bondage to
the first wax imprint made on childhood sensibilities.
One need not be branded by the first pattern.
Once the deforming mirror is smashed,
there is the possibility of wholeness;
there is the possibility of joy.

Life shrinks or expands
in proportion to one's courage.

-Anais Nin

Contents

List of Illustrations

Preface

So you've picked up this book to read - with the hope of what? Maybe finding out what the title means ... who is *The Image Maker?* I'll cut to the chase. The *image maker is* **you!**

Let me give you an example. When you think about your life, your career, your physical image, your relationships – what do you see? Well, what you see is what you get – literally! You probably envisioned yourself exactly as you are right now, "because (you would tell me) that's what is real, that's reality." That vision is the image you hold of yourself *right now.* But is that the image that you want to live with forever?

Is what people see when they look at you the image that you want projected? Your external image is a reflection of your *internal* image. It's like the cover on the book of *You.*

In *The Image Maker,* I'll not only tell you how to change your thinking about yourself and give you practical ways to do so, but I'll help you to discover your inner beauty and talents that already exist - probably lying dormant. It is time to wake them up and discover the true "beautiful you" no matter what your age or no matter what your excuse for not living the life you want to live and deserve to have.

You already have everything you need to begin this journey to the new you. It is time to get moving with your life. *The time is now!*

The Dragonfly

It was suggested to me by a friend that I should elaborate on the relevance of the dragonfly on the cover of this book. She explained that the meaning, if explained up front, could be the very best introduction I could offer as to what lies within these pages.

In nearly every part of the world, the dragonfly symbolizes change and self-realization. It represents mental and emotional maturity and the understanding of the deeper meaning of life. In Japan, dragonflies symbolize good luck and strength. As a creature of the wind, the dragonfly symbolizes change, and like the creature with the delicate wings sensitive to the slightest breeze, we are reminded to go with the flow and catch the updraft.

The name comes from the dragon itself, both of which have been immortalized in mythology all over the world. Historically, the dragonfly was used in love spells. Dragonflies are seen as omens of good luck, particularly if one lands on you. Many pagan cultures saw them as having magical qualities, believing they can travel as messengers between dimensions. According to certain spiritual traditions, dragonflies are thought to be the guides for souls who are revisiting their families on earth.

An ancient, beautiful insect that has been on earth for over 300 million years, there are over 5,000 native species around the world. It is known from fossils, one of which was found in Kansas, that they had wingspans of up to 2 ½ feet.

The life cycle of a dragonfly may be from six months to six years, however, once the nymph sheds its skin, the adult will only live for about two months.

Symbolically, the life of the dragonfly suggests a focus on living in the present moment and making the most of that time.

Moving quickly through life, this is one of the fastest insects, traveling from 40 to 60 mph. With independently jointed wings, it can move backwards, up, down and sideways. Some Native Americans believe it represents swiftness, illusion, and change; and because it is found near sources of water, it is also associated with purity.

The water's surface, where the dragonfly flitters in its natural habitat, is thought to be a realm that is symbolic of our shallow, surface thoughts; it's association with water suggesting the act of looking deeper for the implications and aspects of life beneath the surface. As a symbol of both levels of thought, including dreams and intuition, we can use it to balance the mind between the ego and the soul. This is the reason for its frequent use by spiritual practitioners in meditation practices.

The eyes of the dragonfly allow for a 360-degree view of the world, symbolizing the ability to expand one's spiritual vision and to see beyond the limitation of the human self. The wings and body exhibit iridescence, the property of an object to reflect different colors, and may be associated with self-discovery through the revealing of the reflective real self and the removal of obstacles to the revelation of the innate glowing of the soul.

In Animal Spirit Guides, Chris Luttichau says, "Dragonfly encourages us to see the illusions that define us. Let him guide you to the forgotten part of your soul, so that an understanding of your true self can begin to emerge... Realizing our true potential, in a way that also benefits other people, is the ultimate expression of the power of the dragonfly."

The dragonfly is symbolic of letting go of the past and transforming one's life through awareness and gratitude of beauty, both inner and outer, and through knowledge of the brevity of life and the importance of every moment.

In the pages that follow, I hope that you will find your own depth of beauty and connect with your soul, allowing the transformation to reveal the iridescent you.

Thanks and credits to the following sources of information on the dragonfly:

http://www.allthingshealing.com/Intuition-Symbols/Symbolic-Meaning-of-Dragonfly/7697#.UWHwNRlcRXI
http://daughterofmaat.hubpages.com/hub/All-About-Dragonflies-Dragonfly-Symbolism
http://www.dragonfly-site.com/meaning-symbolize.html
http://www.dragonflysymbolism.com/
http://dragonflyhealing.wordpress.com/2008/12/19/dragonfly-symbolism/

Cover illustration by R. John Ichter
Dragonflies dream
www.ichter.com

Most especially, credit and warm thanks to Bob Ichter for his beautiful artwork that makes up the cover of this book. I will be forever grateful for his generous sharing of his talent.

Please visit his work at: www.Ichter.com and at Belleza Gallery, Bisbee, Arizona, a non profit that supports Renaissance House, a halfway house for homeless women and those recovering from substance abuse and domestic violence. Please visit them online at BellezaGallery.org.

CHAPTER 1

Never Judge a Book by its Cover

Of course, we do this all the time, don't we? We do judge a book by its cover. We all make judgments based on appearances. At a social gathering, we are initially either attracted to or repelled by individuals based on their appearances. When visiting the supermarket, we make purchases according to the impact that packaging has on our psyche with placement on the shelves designed to catch our attention. We are drawn to what is attractive or exciting to our senses, pulled towards that which is beautiful – and we give it credit for other positive attributes by virtue of its possession of beauty.

Advertising and marketing companies spend millions of dollars researching what causes people to buy and they frequently utilize beautiful faces to sell us on the merits of their product. Research has shown that we tend to trust a more attractive person more quickly than a less attractive person.

In an article posted on CNN.com by Kate Lorenz titled "Do Pretty People Earn More?" she tells us:

> According to Dr. Gordon Patzer, who has spent more than three decades studying and writing about physical attractiveness, human beings are hard-wired to respond more favorably to attractive people. Even studies of babies show they will look more intently and longer at prettier faces.

> Studies show attractive students get more attention and higher evaluations from their teachers, good-looking patients get more personalized care from their doctors, and handsome criminals receive lighter sentences than less attractive convicts.

So what *is* beauty? And who is the judge of whom or what is beautiful? Television and film stars and celebrities of all types have personal trainers, makeup artists and hair stylists on staff, as well as publicists whose job it is to "make them look good" in the public eye. The rest of us women, for example, take care of it ourselves with once-a-month hair appointments, department store makeovers, and the continuing hope that we'll eventually lose those 25 extra pounds somewhere out on our morning walk ... and not find them again!

The standards describing what is beautiful or *who* is beautiful have changed throughout history. Twiggy, a very thin, almost boyish looking model with no apparent curves and a short, cropped hairdo to match was the quintessential figure of perfection in the late 1960's. Today we see her as someone who likely had an eating disorder. Some people do find thin females more attractive than more full-figured ones, although today it's easy to find stores with beautiful ads for more voluptuous females - ones who likely never saw a size two since toddlerhood.

Unfortunately it is all too common for adolescent girls to associate thinness as being the ideal and many young girls become concerned about weight to the detriment of their health, not allowing their natural shapes to develop with proper diet and exercise. Although statistically about one third of American children are overweight, there is a national obsession with thinness among teenage girls. They, like many adult women, fail to recognize the importance of health as it relates to the exterior body.

Throughout history, the many changes in hairstyles and makeup have continually re-defined the standards of beauty. Lovers of classic films may find it hard to see what made an actress a beautiful star in her day when we view her through the lens of today's standards. The differences are far greater than hairstyle and makeup.

In 1994, Olympic medalist Dana Torres posed alongside supermodels in the *Sports Illustrated* swimsuit edition, the first time that a female athlete had that distinction. Only a few decades following the Twiggy phenomenon, we have come to value muscles on a woman and an athletic body. A woman can now be strong and sexy. More kudos to Torres because on August 17, 2008 at age 41, she won the silver medal in Beijing, missing the gold by only .01 second in the 50 meter freestyle. Dana had won nine Olympic medals prior to that, and triumphed over women who weren't yet born when she won her earlier medals. So today women are strong, beautiful and in their prime even after 40!

This type of female competition was unheard of just ten years ago, and would have been considered immoral thirty or more years ago. We've definitely come a long way.

Beauty in History

Folklore says that when Marie Antoinette was beheaded in France following the French Revolution of 1789, the makeup on her face was over an inch thick. It has been speculated that she just did not wash her face; make-up was applied on top of many layers of make-up.

In the eighteenth century, the custom was to bathe no more frequently than once a year. Just a hundred years prior, customs dictated a monthly bath for Christians who feared that frequent bathing would rob them of their spirit. However, this was not the case regarding hot springs baths like those at Bath, England, first established by the Romans in approximately 43 C.E. The Romans were famous for their complex bathing systems in all of their territories, but bathing was considered a luxury for the wealthy, to make one more appealing.

The waters at Bath were later blessed by an early Christian monk, and the city became a resort town for the wealthy and privileged during the reign of Elizabeth I. One hundred years later Anglo Christians had moved away from the custom of "frequent" monthly baths to bathing no more than once a year. Obviously, the move was not towards improved hygiene!

It's hard to fathom what impact this hygiene must have had on personal appearances, not to mention personal relationships. While amusing in a repugnant way, we can easily see how ideas have changed about what is considered desirable. They seem to fluctuate and cycle just as fashions have. A standing joke with women is that if you hang on to something long enough, it will come back into fashion (case in point are wide bottom jeans, known in the 60's as "bell bottoms")!

The feminist movement, which began in the sixties, espoused freedom from many tyrannical notions of femininity and beauty. It was a time when many of us abandoned our bras, lipsticks and razors, and this didn't always make for a pretty picture! Many relevant and positive changes came out of that movement. Gloria Steinem, a pioneer in the feminist movement said about popular trends in feminine attire:

For women... bras, panties, bathing suits, and other stereotypical gear are visual reminders of a commercial, idealized feminine image that our real and diverse female bodies can't possibly fit. Without these visual references, each individual woman's body demands to be accepted on its own terms. We stop being comparatives. We begin to be unique.

Nonetheless, lingerie is as popular as ever with Victoria's Secret Angels promoting sexy beauty. Similarly, cosmetics is another multi-billion dollar industry.

We hear often that "beauty is in the eye of the beholder." Very few women have "perfectly proportioned" figures, and if we refer back just a few paragraphs, we know that ideal proportions change with time and the styles of the day. In the 1960's, icon Marilyn Monroe was a size 14!

So what is it that determines *who* is beautiful?

CHAPTER 2

Seeing is Believing

If it's true that "beauty is in the eye of the beholder," then how is it that many people will disagree on who *is* beautiful?

It's a matter of *perception*.

Perception is one's point-of-view on any particular topic. The idea that we see the glass as either half-empty (pessimistically) or half-full (optimistically) is a reflection of our perception. Our perceptions include all of our opinions and attitudes on every conceivable subject, including our perception of *ourselves*. Perception is a pattern or habit. We see ourselves how we've been trained to see ourselves and others.

So if our perceptions are habitual, does that mean that we're stuck with them? Or can they be changed – molded into something more in line with what we desire for our lives? The good news is that they *can* be changed, and that is what this book is all about. I will teach you how to accomplish this (it will be up to you to *do* it, though).

The old adage, "beauty is only skin-deep" is so very profound. This cliché is most often used as a negative statement that a beautiful woman or anything of "beauty" may have underlying traits that aren't so pretty. A rose has a thorn. It is a "sticking point." The same goes for humans. We are all made up of beauty *and* the things we'd rather prune from our lives. This book will help you identify what needs to be pruned from your life to help the beauty, your true underlying beauty to emerge and blossom. Although our external reality or the way we look is important, it's only a small fraction of what needs to change in order to allow your inner beauty to shine and for you to develop an image that expresses who you truly are. You are valuable in any state. But too often we can't find the way to feel our worth, much less to express it externally.

I have just introduced you to the key concept in creating the life and the image that you desire for the rest of the world to see. There are internal processes that go on within each of us that dictate how we see ourselves and how much we buy into the mass marketing of sexuality and what is beautiful. Inside each and every one of us is the ability and the power to make our life whatever we want it to be. So it's an "inside job," as one wise friend of mine says. By the way, if the people around you don't think like this, you may want to consider expanding your inner circle to include those who do – I call this your "circle of influence." Those around you do affect the way you see yourself, so ask yourself this, "Who in my circle makes me feel good about myself when I'm around them? Who doesn't?" Notice how do you feel the "vibes" you get from each of them?

Almost from the moment we arrive here on planet earth, we are taught to observe and to trust in our five senses. Our senses inform our minds what is happening around us, and this obviously critical information is used to function and be safe in the physical world. We are raised to listen and to watch and to be obedient to our parents and teachers. We are told how things work and we take it on faith, never questioning the motives or perceptions of those who teach us. How could we even begin to question anything? We know nothing but what we've learned thus far – we have no basis for comparison.

Our earliest experiences are the *norm*. Furthermore, the norm becomes *our* norm. This is called conditioning and we have *all* been conditioned. Not one of us escapes it. Our automatic responses to situations have been imprinted upon us in early childhood, at a time when we were like little dry sponges, soaking up information at a phenomenal speed. We don't recognize this conditioning because it is deeply imprinted on us at a level that cannot be accessed consciously. It is in our subconscious mind, below the level of our awareness. And no amount of trying to access it makes any difference. If it seems like I'm painting a dismal picture here, bear with me, as I will put it all into perspective a bit later in Chapter 9: "Re-Programming Your Self" (if you just can't wait).

I am trying to show here that our perception of ourselves and everything around us has been conditioned to a point where we don't recognize that something we accepted as true might not be true at all. You may have a negative self-image because someone told you that you were ugly or fat or uncoordinated as a child. Just because someone said it, that doesn't make it so. I want you to just begin to play with the idea that you may believe things that are false, especially about yourself, your beauty, your worth and your abilities. And that can be changed with a little bit of work and education on the subject.

So far I've told you that your power resides within you, then contradicted that by telling you that you have been conditioned and, furthermore, that you can't even find out exactly what that conditioning entails. How can I suggest that these contradictory states can be resolved? Because I know that we are something much greater than what many of us have been raised to believe that we are. We are not just limited human beings graced with a soul. We are spiritual beings graced with a body.

Since we are spiritual beings, having a physical experience, we have been gifted with an intellect to bridge the gap between the physical and the non-physical worlds - between our reality and our dreams.

If this idea is new to you, then there are no cells of recognition with which to process and assimilate this information, because the process of introducing a new intellectual concept sometimes rattles the cage of our paradigms- or our models for life. This is a primary way in which we discover what conditioning resides within our subconscious mind. Our discomfort at entertaining the new idea reveals a paradigm, our pattern of thinking. Up until now our choices and our actions have been quietly directed by this pattern. Now the noise begins with the introduction of this unfamiliar idea.

A client I'll call Susan, to protect her confidentiality, was desperately unhappy with her life and her appearance. She lived alone and had recently given up her only friendship around the time that we began working together. She felt isolated and lonely and frequently angry. Despite her seemingly high level of motivation to change her life, Susan's even higher level of fear of the unknown controlled her to the extent that she couldn't entertain new ways of being. Every week we were back to the same place processing the same issues again. Susan was looping through the same material week after week because she was afraid to experience any discomfort long enough to create a new pattern of being, which included new ways of thinking about herself and how life *could* be.

Repetition is the key to learning. A belief is only a thought that has been rehearsed enough times that it assumes the status of a "belief." Exposure to a new idea with consistent attention given to it will provide the opportunity to create new beliefs. Learning how to do something for the first time, then practicing it repeatedly until totally absorbed in the process, will eventually lead to the new idea becoming second nature. With persistence, Susan could have had a different life with a changed paradigm that would have facilitated *lasting* change.

Changing our perception requires a conscious effort on our part. We have to retrain ourselves to first see our beauty as we are, yet remain committed to taking steps to self improvement. And that begins with letting go of some ideas that may not have served your self-awareness over the years. Negative thought patterns confuse us and hold us back. By creating new paradigms, we can create new ways of looking at a new and beautiful self - no matter where your starting point is. Almost everyone's image of themselves can stand to be improved.

CHAPTER 3

Who Are You? Getting Centered

Does evidence exist which points to the idea of us as *spiritual beings*? I would answer with a resounding YES! First we have to examine the ways in which we explain the world, the universe, and our existence- it is referred to as our "cosmology." Basically, it boils down to two very broad and diverse schools of thought. One is the scientific approach and the other is the theological. Both attempt to explain who we are, why we are here and who or what created our existence in this vast, ever expanding universe.

In regards to theology, I'm speaking of all of the world's religious and metaphysical explanations and systems of belief. The majority of these have been monotheistic. There is one God and It is the divine creator of all that is, operating in accordance with spiritual laws. We may refer to this divine creator as *God, Jehovah, Yahweh, Allah, Krishna, Brahma, Buddha, Source, Spirit, Infinite Intelligence, Universe* or *Universal Mind;* these are just a few of the many names that it has been called over the ages.

The theological view of life tends to include one common tendency, regardless of religion, and that is the exercise of *faith.* Faith is the belief in something intangible. In other words, we believe without concrete proof in something or someone. Without faith, the theological or religious system has no substance.

While the continued cultivation of active faith is a lifelong process, a fundamental faith is necessary in order to maintain a core belief in the tenets of that belief system — *faith* is even the name of *where* we have placed our spiritual faith, as in, "I am of the Catholic faith."

In contrast to the theological approach to understanding the cosmos and our place in it, the scientific approach to understanding the universe does not require faith. An inquiring mind and critical thinking are the backbone of scientific discoveries, although it must also involve a creative imagination to perceive the existence of that which hasn't yet been discovered or proven. A scientist must be able to prove his hypothesis through consistent replication of the experiment or "empirical data," achieving exactly identical results every time. This is referred to as "inductive reasoning" or "the scientific method." The persistence and perseverance required to pursue answers to natural phenomena occurring at an invisible level, however, certainly requires some degree of faith.

Quantum physics is the scientific study of matter, energy, force and motion, and the way they relate to each other, particularly as applied to the smallest unit or quantity of a physical property. What is unarguably understood thus far is that there is a vast universe about which we understand very little. We do know, however, that at the smallest level of matter, it isn't matter at all but waves of energy that are like packets of potentialities. This energy makes up the spaces around the existing matter as a field of potentiality. Furthermore, the energy in this field responds to human consciousness and the act of expectant observation, by changing from energy waves to particles, or quanta. German born Max Planck was awarded the Nobel Prize in 1918 for this paradigm-shifting discovery of the smallest unit of matter. He was quoted as saying, "If we change the way we look at things, the things we look at change." The implications of this statement and the discovery behind it are profound. It means that energy literally becomes matter and takes *form* according to *our thoughts*. As Mike Dooley emphasizes on the hit DVD *The Secret*, "Thoughts become things!" It also implies that our thoughts are the most powerful form of energy in the universe, capable of creating *something from nothing*. Actually, our thoughts create from the existing energy fields around us, especially those on the subatomic level. Energy will always exist. It can neither be created nor destroyed; but it can be reshaped.

In her book *The Field*, Lynn McTaggert provides an exhaustive compilation of all the relevant studies from scientific research. She refers to the empty spaces around matter as the "zero point field." It is in this field that life is teeming with potentiality awaiting human consciousness to birth it into physical existence. Not only is it the source of an infinite number of possibilities yet to be conceived, but the field is also the repository of every idea that has ever existed, *and* every subsequent event that ever proceeded from those ideas. This shared collection of information gathered from everybody who has ever lived, may be the source of inspired thought or intelligence accessible to each and every one of us. If we also consider that all that is *unknown* is included in this same field, then would it be a huge jump to think of this space as a greater "Mind"? And what if we are each connected to it through our own minds?

This information may seem a bit heavy so let's put it in simplified form. What are some examples of ways that we use our thoughts to create something that we *intend* or want to bring into our lives? Though most of us want to create our first (or second or third) million dollars right now, a dream car or the ultimate romantic relationship, it is much easier to do this using smaller ideas that we can then build upon with practice. For example, imagine attracting a free cup of coffee, tea or cocktail - whatever it is you would like to sip right now. Set your intention to attract that. Imagine yourself receiving this "gift" from the universe. Sooner or later a friend will call, or you'll stop at your favorite coffee shop and someone may offer to pay for your order. I know a man who once paid for the entire fast food order of the person in the car behind him. He kept telling me, "I don't know what made me do it. I couldn't even see who was in the car!" It may well have been a case of someone in the other car intending abundance in their life, manifesting it as a gift from a stranger! (I also love that he was open to listening to that message!)

Or this is another favorite pastime of mine. Think of an old friend or relative who you've lost touch with and would like to reconnect. Focus on hearing from that person. Write their name down and focus on what they look like, what they sound like, and the joy their presence brings into your life. The energy will shift in order to draw that person back into your life; someone may bring up their name and know how to contact them, or they may just reach out to you. It's a lot of fun to practice and we begin to learn how to create the larger things we want to attract!

Buckminster Fuller, who was one of the world's greatest thinkers said, "Everyone is born a genius, but the process of living de-geniuses them." What Fuller means here is that we all have this capability of manifesting our greatest desires, but because of the often negative teachings we've been subjected to - which shaped our existing paradigms - we've forgotten how to create. Instead we limit ourselves to lack and scarcity, sometimes in all areas of our life— including simple joy. Unfortunately, many of us have learned to be sad and depressed because that is what we think we deserve. That is one of those paradigms I intend to show you how to let go of in this book. Because suffering and depression will create more suffering and depression.

The material or medium of the zero point field provides a means of communication between everything that exists. This communication occurs at the subatomic level as a *vibration*. *Everything* vibrates. The universe is in constant motion and expanding but the rate of frequency or the speed is so rapid that it is imperceptible to our physical senses. Otherwise, we would see that matter is flashing in and out of existence. Actually, as it flashes in and out of existence it's imperceptibly changing shape, but as mentioned before, the energy is never destroyed. The effect is much the same as a motion picture series of photographic frames that flow continuously and appear as real as life. A great analogy is that our minds are the silver screens of this long-running movie that we each call our *life*.

Our cells and our DNA communicate because of and through these frequencies. Consequently, our bodies are in constant relationship with the environment, as subatomic particles within are continually exchanged with the environment. Those who define existence through scientific understanding may simply refer to this organizing, unifying force as *energy*. We are truly connected to everything and everyone else, despite our individual experience as an isolated being. In other words, we are not isolated "down here" with the Creator being separate and distant from us "out there." I contend, along with countless others, that we are connected through energy. The quantum physicists call this entanglement. The Buddhists call it oneness.

Today, there is a convergence between science and spirituality. The overlap is due to our quest for understanding of this world we live in. The discovery of subatomic particles and their characteristic constant flux provides scientific validation to the ancient Eastern sages' teachings on the transient nature of all things. Seeking answers to life's questions has led many scientists to ascribe cause to an organized intelligence, as Max Planck's research led him to state: "We must assume behind this force the existence of a conscious and intelligent mind. This mind is the matrix of all matter."

Regardless of the school of thought you subscribe to — scientific or theological, energy or spirit, and it may be a bit of both — I propose to you that who we really are is first and foremost a spiritual or energetic being. For the sake of consistency in all future references I will use the term *spiritual* being. I am hopeful that, by the end of this chapter, you will have come to a new understanding and awareness of who you are.

The Stickperson

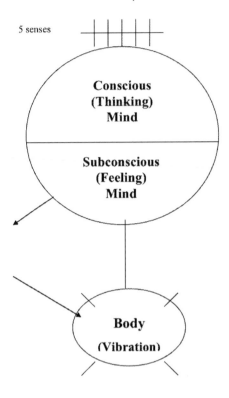

5 senses

**Conscious
(Thinking)
Mind**

**Subconscious
(Feeling)
Mind**

Body

(Vibration)

In the 1930's, a holistic chiropractor from San Antonio, Texas, developed a way to look at the human mind through the illustration called the "The Magical Graphic." Dr. Thurman Fleet was attempting to teach his patients about the functioning of body-mind-spirit and realized that he needed a visual presentation of the mind if he was going to be able to communicate about it, since our minds think in pictures. He developed what later came to be known as "Concept Therapy" and came up with the Stickperson drawing that you see here. We'll use the top circle to represent the mind, and the smaller one to represent the body, and we'll divide the top circle into two hemispheres. The top half will represent the conscious mind and the lower half the subconscious mind.

The Mind

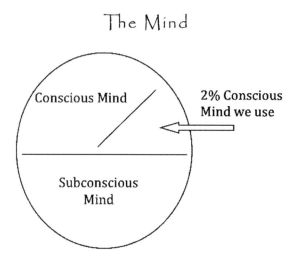

Now let's begin with your birth. You are born into a physical world and you learn to navigate it through the use of your physical senses. You gather data from your experiences, your parents and other significant people in your life, and from influences in the media. All of that data is stored in your subconscious mind, which essentially functions as a storage receptacle that is primarily focused on your survival. Until around school age, this part of the mind is all that we possess to operate with. It's also important to understand that the subconscious mind does not possess the capacity to discriminate what is impressed upon it. Every experience is stored equally. However, a predominance of similar experiences together will form dominant influences or conditioning. In other words, if a child experiences happiness and joy most of the time, it will learn to be happy, but if she experiences lots of sadness, pain and discomfort, she will very likely perceive that mindset as normal. The subconscious mind holds and maintains what you believe about yourself. It is the seat of your self-image, according to Maxwell Maltz, in *Psycho-cybernetics*. The early Greeks referred to this part of us as *sanctum sanctorum,* or our "heart of hearts."

Neuroscience has revealed that there is an emotional component to our memories, suggesting that they are stored *because* of their emotional content. Because of this, the subconscious mind is also referred to as the Emotional or Feeling Mind. The contents of the subconscious mind are responsible for our ever-changing feelings. We have stored a lifetime of emotional experiences. Early experiences that were similar in nature formed systems of belief or *paradigms*. This is the conditioning that was mentioned earlier, and the habitual nature of the subconscious mind creates an automatic response to whatever the mind considers to be a relevant trigger. Therefore, you can be going along and minding your own business, so to speak, when suddenly you're washed over with a flood of feelings that seem to come out of nowhere, overwhelming in their intensity and sometimes leading to inexplicable or irrational behaviors. *"What just happened?"* your conscious mind may ask, but there is no answer forthcoming. Something has triggered a subconscious memory through emotional association and the feeling triggered an automatic behavioral response through your autonomic nervous system (ANS). This conditioned response is designed to protect you and perpetuate your survival, but it isn't always appropriate to the current situation. Although you may know better, you may find yourself struggling to do the right thing or to make sense of self-destructive impulses or compulsive behaviors. If you know what you need to do, then why don't you just do it? That is the power of the subconscious mind with its habitual conditioned responses – the paradigm running your life.

Results

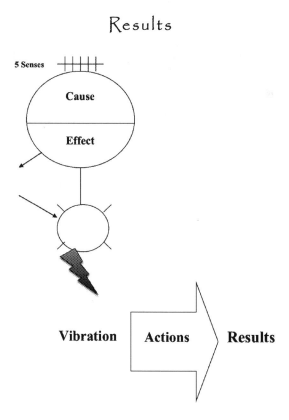

Our subconscious mind also runs the functioning of our physical body. It is the rate of frequency, or our *vibration*, that determines our actions. We experience these vibrations as our *feelings*. There is a direct correlation between our feelings and our behavior – they are flip sides of the same coin. Our feelings, or vibrational frequency, dictate our physical actions. Our actions resonate with our feelings. This resonance is the essence of the *Law of Attraction*. It is often phrased as "what we think about we bring about," or "thoughts become things."

If you'll think about the last time you were feeling especially good, you'll probably recall that there was a spring in your step, a smile on your face and your head was held high. You'll also likely recall that your good feelings seemed to be met with mostly positive reactions from those you encountered. This is the Law of Attraction at work – *like attracts like* - another way to understand this fundamental universal law.

Until about six years old, we operate without a sense of real identity. Around the time we start school, we develop the capacity for objective thinking. Scientist and philosopher René Descartes said, "I think, therefore I am." That is the essence of the conscious mind.

The conscious mind is the Thinking Mind, and it has the capacity to accept, reject or neglect any idea or thought presented to it. Now this ability grows over time, but is never fully developed without intentional effort. Many adults function with the same thinking capacity that they were operating with when they were ten or twelve years old. Ideally, our early twenties is a great time to begin to cultivate our thinking capacity for consciously navigating this journey through life.

We have been equipped with an Intellectual Mind, a deeper aspect of the thinking mind that, according to Napoleon Hill, operates through six fundamental faculties. Hill, author of the classic *Think and Grow Rich,* devoted 25 years of his life to studying the 500 richest and most powerful men in the world. (At that time no women were being credited with having broken through that paradigm – regardless if any had!) Hill uncovered thirteen fundamental values that they all agreed upon, as well as the existence of these intellectual faculties: Persistence, Will, Imagination, Intuition, Memory and Reason. It is not until one becomes introduced to the idea of developing these intellectual faculties that it might even occur to them to function outside the realm of the five physical senses. Without the conscious use of these faculties I refer to this as *taking life by default* - like going through life on automatic pilot, or just rolling the dice, taking what life dishes out - occasionally protesting fate but never realizing how or *what* is producing the results.

We're conditioned to do this. How many times have you heard someone say, "Let's just wait and see what happens"? This is relegating control of one's life to … to what? To nothing. Do you recall our earlier discussion - that human consciousness is responsible for the creation of matter from the field of potentiality? There is no life *out there*. The only life there is belongs to you, and is *in you*.

So let's get back to our Stickperson. We have the large circle on top designed to represent our mind. The conscious mind thinks about an idea or perceives some sensory information and passes it through to the subconscious mind where it is stored as a feeling; this feeling vibration has a certain rate of frequency which determines the subsequent action, and the actions ultimately leads to some result. So, in brief:

Thoughts lead to Feelings; Feelings lead to Actions; and Actions produce Results.

The Cycle of Results

Next in our typical thought processes we evaluate our results, usually by perceiving it through one or more of our five senses and then thinking about it. This elicits and activates an old feeling, and the feeling-vibration leads to the next round of action. Then we evaluate those results and make the next decision, and so on. The problem is that we look at our results and oftentimes draw erroneous conclusions. The evaluation we conduct is usually based upon our memory of a similar experience from the past. This may or may not be an appropriate match, although it usually works in the area of general functioning, such as with driving. If you see the taillights on the vehicle in front of you suddenly light up, it IS a good idea to apply your brakes immediately, which is something that you've learned to do. On the flip side, if you experience a hostile situation in which you would normally raise your voice and enter into a verbal battle, and you've learned that this reaction usually just escalates into heightened negative emotions and anger, then maybe there is a better choice of reaction. You might even recognize your reactivity and see the opportunity to be pro-active instead, pre-determining a better course of action. But usually when we perform a self-evaluation we'll pull from old conditioning which involves habitual self-limiting beliefs. This can only lead to erroneous conclusions which can then only lead to erroneous decision-making. This is an example of a self-limiting belief in operation.

A young woman I'll call Mary had been raised in an emotionally abusive home; she experienced many years of harsh criticism and was the sole object of her mother's ridicule and attacks. This abuse was compounded by a disengaged father who listened to her mother's tirades about her and oftentimes doled-out the punishment. When Mary first came to see me, her anxiety level was so high that she could barely function any longer at her job. The stressors in her life had taken such a toll on her coping resources that when she experienced conflict at work her automatic reaction was to expect that "they were out to get her." The lifelong conditioning from her abusive family life had her convinced that everyone at work was in conspiratorial agreement that she was "no good" and they were going to get rid of her. If she saw a couple of co-workers involved in a private conversation, Mary was certain that they were talking about her. She used her sensory factors to gather data, but the conditioning within her subconscious mind created erroneous deductions, leading to false assumptions and self-damaging conclusions. Despite what evidence she had to the contrary, it took years of confronting this paradigm before she was able to begin to see it from a different perspective. She eventually learned to talk herself down from the ledge and to find and connect with a better-feeling thought, which created an entirely different and much more satisfying outcome.

So if we want different results, we must retrace our steps backwards from our current results and look at the processes that led up to that outcome. Today's results are a reflection of what you have been thinking up until now. If you don't *know* what you've been thinking – just look at your current results! For example, another client I'll call Emily couldn't understand why she was feeling so much frustration with her nine-year old daughter. She reported that ever since her daughter had been a toddler, she had always been difficult to deal with. Emily reported to me that she would start out feeling patient, but as her daughter acted-up, her own feelings would escalate. They would end up in a power struggle, with Emily finally losing her patience and yelling at her daughter. Although still frustrated, Emily would feel guilty and ultimately end up not following through with the consequence she had assigned. This reaction, in turn, led to more feelings of guilt of not being a good [i.e. consistent] parent. And here is the crux of the story: her guilt evoked memories of her own mother who she had disliked, and her driving fear was that her own daughter disliked her in the same way. This fear stood in the way of her responding spontaneously and creatively, and in attuned relationship with her child. Instead, she was operating from fear and the imagined dread of her own daughter's dislike of her – repeating the pattern in this family AND creating the very thing which she did NOT want to happen. Like attracts like. When we think good, life-affirming thoughts, we get more of those. And when we think negative, fearful, energy-depleting thoughts, we get more of those too! Her thoughts created a feeling (vibration) within her that attracted more of that same feeling (vibration) and caused her to behave in a manner consistent with those feelings, leading to more of the same.

Descartes is quoted as saying, "Insanity is repeating the same behavior over and over again, all the while expecting a different result." We are all familiar with Emily's experience – what we're doing isn't working, so we "up the ante" and do more of it. Yelling didn't work so we yell a little louder until finally we're screaming. Of course, that doesn't work either and then we feel stuck and lost, with no idea of what to do next.

This is where the Intellectual Faculties come to our rescue. These faculties are really what separate us from the animals. We have been endowed with the capacity to think *beyond* our conditioning – to think creatively. We are able to connect with and draw upon our Spiritual Mind or energy through the use of our Intuition. Wayne Dyer said, "If prayer is us communing with God, then intuition is God communicating with us." We must develop our intuitive faculties until we are able to hear that small, still voice within us that gives us the answers. Our Perception will reveal our point-of-view; our glass is either half empty or half full. We want to develop the ability to evaluate circumstances in the light of what we *want* to see. Then we can Reason our way through the problem, rejecting whatever thoughts do not lead to better feelings, and focusing on those that do. Our Imagination can serve us by presenting new and creative solutions; and our Will must be exercised to concentrate and focus, and to direct our imagination away from worst-case scenarios. And our Memory, plentifully loaded with examples of prior failings in similar circumstances, must be managed through our Reason and our Will to instead provide examples of previous successes.

This is a brief description of the use of the Intellectual Faculties to exercise our intention to create the life we desire. More will be said later, although a full chapter or even a book could easily be written on each one of these faculties.

In summary, the assumption has been made that we are spiritual beings who have the ability to create the life we desire and that this life is of our own creation. What has this got to do with our image? Everything!

Who we *think* we are comes out of our conditioned mind. Who have *you* been conditioned to think you are? Are you expressing *your* unique potential?

CHAPTER 4

What Other People Think of You
is None of Your Business

You wouldn't worry what others thought of you if you realized how seldom they do. That's because *everyone's* favorite topic is *them self.* Unless they are being personally affected, most people will give only passing attention to the subject of another person, habitually returning to their own concerns. This suggests the strong possibility that others' thoughts of you probably revolve around what they think that *you* think of *them*!

How can we make it this far down the road of life and still be worrying about what other people are thinking about us? You may feel that this discussion doesn't apply to you because you've overcome such concerns, but I propose to you that this process is insidiously subtle. It's hidden away in those deep recesses of your subconscious mind and shows up when you least expect it. It's all part of our conditioning or programming, our paradigms. We don't even notice that to which we are so accustomed. If everyone in your universe had blonde hair, would you even notice the color of anyone's hair? The same is true with societal or behavioral norms. We notice that which deviates from the norm (*not-blonde* would create sudden awareness) because it is outside the paradigm where no "cells of recognition" exist.

These are cells or neural patterns that form at the time of a new experience, creating a reference point for future recognition. They also serve for *generalizing* other experiences, which is a mental process that allows for efficient functioning. But oftentimes it creates obstacles to learning because we might not entertain a new experience if it seems familiar - we may believe it to be a repeat of a similar earlier experience and so we may dismiss the new information.

With all these mental activities going on underground, it's no wonder that we don't recognize the routine daily patterns of our thoughts. We have grown up in households within neighborhoods, inside communities or cities where we have been exposed to and molded by the dominant cultural influences including the religious, political and other moral bases that have formed our ideas of what is right or wrong. What people think of us establishes each one of us within that community and determines how we will be treated. The role of parents is to develop their children into members of their society who will be respected and will prosper. "Good-enough" parents are those who, for the most part, sufficiently meet their children's needs and want them to be happy and secure. There is a survival instinct at work here. The success of one becomes the success of all. All this occurs at a mostly subconscious level. We instinctually repeat this behavior with our own children, as they will with theirs. It's how our culture is perpetuated and our survival in that community is secured. Children who grow up in farming communities often feel the need to plant a garden, even in a small space, in order to produce at least a portion of their food. And those parents who emphasized the importance of team sports with their children usually are at the soccer or baseball field watching their grandchildren play. Families who own businesses raise children who are frequently entrepreneurial. An even greater example is that of "political families" in which members from many generations are involved in the political system, such as the Kennedys and the Bushes. Even hobbies are often perpetuated over generations.

So we see that this isn't an accidental process but one based on the instinctive perpetuation of the species, sometimes to maintain a sense of power or status. That may sound like an over-dramatization, but I want to make the point that the messages received by a child are delivered with a certain intensity and they continue throughout their life. The earliest years, however, find the most fertile soil in a young child's mind. There is no filter of self-consciousness in place yet and all input is received equally and becomes permanently stored. These impressions cumulatively form what becomes the *self-image*. The subconscious mind, lacking the ability to discriminate or reject any thought impressed upon it, creates clusters of ideas according to the nature of the idea and the emotions attached.

This is the foundation of a paradigm. The strength of the paradigm is dependent upon the preponderance of that idea. In other words, a repeating theme in the messages received by that child will lead to the creation of a strong paradigm. Being told once that you're stupid doesn't impact the mind if it's a somewhat isolated incident. Repeatedly being told this has the power to become a dominant paradigm. That paradigm will impact that child's self-image causing them to believe that they lack adequate intelligence. They will believe that they are stupid.

The job of parents is to raise self-sufficient and self-reliant adults. There are essentially eighteen years to get the job done. However, a major part of that work is completed within the first six years. The rest of the time is spent reinforcing the earlier messages. Corrections can be made down the road, and the earlier the better. The most effective corrections are ideally delivered by the primary caretakers (the ones who delivered the original messages) and the sooner the better.

In my therapy practice, the recurring theme with every client is the relationship with the parents. Fair or not, the relationship with mother is the pivotal one, even if she was absent. This relationship starts during the time in-utero when the developing fetus is directly connected to their mother's body and feelings. This is the *first relationship*, the one that sets the tone for every other relationship the child will ever have. It is the prototype or the model on which all other relationships are formed. Regardless of the quality or nature of that relationship, it constitutes the child's first impression and experience of how she will be treated and dictates what she expects and hopes for in terms of getting her own needs met. The term "good enough mothering" implies that no mother is perfect, but if she mostly responds to and meets the child's physical and emotional needs in a timely manner, then there is a strong likelihood that the child will develop into a well-adjusted individual. She will become a person who knows how to trust and will expect the world to treat her with sufficient regard. She will have a secure internal attachment.

What if you weren't raised with good-enough mothering, let alone with positive, confidence-producing messages? What if the majority of the things you heard were fear-based, negative or critical, and now you find yourself sensitive to others' thoughts and opinions of you? There comes a time in everyone's life when they must decide for themselves what will be the beliefs and core values that will direct their life. It's a coming-of-age, so to speak, and it can happen at any time along the road of life, but frequently occurs around our early 40's. Our society recognizes this as a "mid-life crisis," too often characterized by a divorce and a flashy new car (nothing wrong with either one of those, as long as they're not the "fix" for a broken or empty life). Discovering what *we* want is what creates meaning in our life and launches us onto our uniquely individual path. It can be either the most exciting or most frustrating challenge of adulthood.

How can we find out what our core values are? We can start with examining what we currently believe. Identify what *doesn't resonate* with your being, but instead is creating a feeling of disharmony or dissonance. Try this experiment: Think of an idea that is unmistakably pleasurable – observe how you feel inwardly; notice the contentment or peacefulness. Next, think of something that you disagree with or dislike and notice the associated feelings, possibly anxiety or maybe even fear. The latter feelings reflect dissonance and are useful in pointing you in the opposite direction and towards what *will* resonate. Oftentimes we don't know what we want, but we do know what we *don't* want. We can use that which we don't want as a starting point in our discovery: *I know I don't want to go through life feeling that I'm not making any difference in the world; therefore, finding a way to serve will be more gratifying for me.* Identifying what we want is a gradual process of defining and refining and is the driving activity of life. It is often helpful to write down that which resonates and that which does not, creating categories as such. We can then "see" what we want and what we don't want. We can then focus on what we *want*!

Our desires are what keep us engaged in life. When the day comes that we no longer desire anything, our time on this earth will be drawing to a close. It is an expanding universe and our desires create continued expansion as we seek and push outward. It's our passion in pursuit of our desires that generates a life of meaning and joy. When we know what we want then we can live with the idea that others may not approve or understand what we're doing. Despite someone's disapproval of your choices, it doesn't really matter because their comments indicate only a momentary thought about you and your situation. For example, if they don't support your decision to buy a new car it may be because they feel that *they don't* need (*deserve*) a brand new car, not recognizing their own worth and being jealous. In a different kind of example, it's an odd phenomenon that the same people who may be critical of an alcoholic for their addiction will sometimes resent that person's recovery when it takes away their basis of comparison and their judgment that, "… at least I'm not *that* bad."

We develop tolerance and compassion towards others as we learn that we are each on our own journey and that no one, but us, can decide what's right for us. Despite our conditioning to conform to family or society, eventually we wake up to the fact that all the adults aren't necessarily right. Once we realize that we're one of the adults, we can then begin to question the status quo. Our obedience to authority has cost us our creative ingenuity – coloring inside the lines has created a lot of sameness. What if we went *outside* the lines? Who made the lines in the first place? And what if there *were* no lines? Just the act of exploring and questioning the truths of our lives will lead to an expanded awareness of the possibilities. The question is posed: **Is that the truth, or is it just what you believe?**

Don't accept what you've been told without examining it. Begin to question everything. What we call thinking is in actuality merely the repetition of a previous thought. According to Charlie Greer, author of *What Are You Thinking?* ...... the National Science Foundation put out some very interesting statistics.

The average person thinks about twelve thousand thoughts per day. A deeper thinker ... puts forth fifty thousand thoughts daily.

The majority of these thoughts are mundane and recycled from one day to the next. Deciding to have another cup of coffee or remembering to pick up the dry cleaning does not qualify as critical thinking. Even the glorified *multi-tasking* doesn't make the cut; recent studies are showing that there may be a decrease in mental functioning associated with long-term mental juggling. Newly released results of scientific studies in multitasking indicate that carrying on several duties at once may, in fact, reduce productivity, not increase it.

> "In some cases, you could be wasting your employer's time," says researcher Joshua Rubinstein, Ph.D., formerly of the University of Michigan and now with the Federal Aviation Administration (FAA) working on security issues. "And in certain cases [of multitasking]," Rubinstein says, "you could be risking employers a dangerous outcome." It appears it is time for us all to slow down and really examine our priorities.

We have all been born as unique individuals, each endowed with our own talents and desires. When we don't exercise these talents and abilities, we waste them – they are lost to the rest of the world. We may be holding onto one single idea that has the power to change another person's life. By not bringing it forth, we not only deprive the world of that idea, but we deprive ourselves of the pure act of creation. If we can shift our perspective from worrying about ourselves and how we'll be perceived, to focusing instead on serving others, we'll be able to flow gracefully into the creative mode. Our imagination is the greatest gift we possess. Renown as history's most prolific inventor with 1093 patents to his credit, Thomas Edison had carved into the top of his wooden desk, "Imagination is more powerful than knowledge." He knew that without imagination, knowledge would never expand and would only continue to recycle the existing ideas. We can tap into the storehouse of ideas by connecting with the source of all ideas - the Universe or universal consciousness - God! Becoming quiet and finding solitude and silence within is an essential first step. Contemplation, meditation and prayer are all inwardly directed activities that will still the overactive conscious mind and allow inspired ideas to bubble up and into awareness. We can learn how to tap into this storehouse through various forms of meditation. There are many forms, whether through yoga or Transcendental Meditation© which is where my own journey started. But several years ago, I found my spiritual teacher, Durga Ma, who teaches an ancient form from shaktipat kundalini yoga called Surrender Meditation. She has spent her entire life meditating, studying, and transcribing the Bhagavad Gita. She has written many books and teaches online an interpretation of the Gita that is understandable to westerners. Surrender Meditation, also called full surrender Natural Meditation, requires no will power and is effortless and spontaneous. I incorporate Durga Ma's teachings in my own Mindful Life Mastery coaching program. You can learn more about Durga Ma at www. PhoenixMetaphysical.com or at www.DurgaMa.com.

Meditation allows us to be active in our creativity by becoming passive with our thoughts. Taking the time to still your mind will stimulate your creativity and open you up to a multitude of ideas that could not otherwise come through because your mind was too "busy." When that happens, don't question its value or validity – trust it as the answer to your expectant desire, and run with it. The universe loves speed and where attention goes, energy flows. Allow it to grow without second-guessing its worth and you will experience the absolute joy of creation.

CHAPTER 5

You Don't Get a Second Chance to Make a First Impression

We're all familiar with the expression, "Never judge a book by its cover." Yet who can honestly say that they don't do it? Within the first two to three seconds of meeting someone for the first time, we have sized them up. It's a miraculous process, considering that in the blink of an eye, we have taken in visual, auditory and maybe even olfactory information, registered it and come to our conclusion about that person. All this takes place in the subconscious mind and the final analysis is delivered to our conscious mind, complete with a feeling. We're either attracted or repelled. Sometimes we're indifferent, but this may just reflect a lack of generalized information about people of this "type" by which to categorize this new person. This rarely happens, however, because the mind has a highly developed capacity to generalize and categorize. Generally we either like or dislike someone pretty quickly, without really knowing why.

So what can we do to make the most desirable first impression, knowing that fates are decided within moments of a meeting? First, we need to understand what's involved in the assessment process and even more relevant, why it happens. Earlier I discussed the preservation instinct of an individual within a community. In prehistoric societies, fitting-in was a matter of life or death. We have a survival instinct for getting along with the clan, to insure our getting a warm corner of the cave and a piece of the mammoth. We still don't want to be left out in the cold or be hungry. We are hard-wired to need each other, as well as to compete with others for our individual survival. Many thousands of generations of humanity have performed this same dance and only those who learned the steps survived – the survival of the fittest.

In prehistoric society it's likely there were few choices about the members of one's clan. Today, however, we're more mobile and with social media our reach is expanded and so we have many choices. You might be wondering why this is important? What does it matter who I hang around with if I'm my own person and doing my own thing? A wise person once said, "Your success in life will be a reflection of the books you have read and the people with whom you have associated."

Who do you associate with in your job or business, or personal social life? Probably it's those with whom you feel most comfortable, secure or safe, and quite likely it's someone who makes you feel good. For dysfunctional personalities, it's people to whom they feel superior. But for healthy individuals it is people whose presence makes us feel good. Isn't that really what it's all about, when it's all said and done? You want to feel good, and you'll gravitate to those who make you feel that way. Even when sharing things in common such as similar incomes, possessions, and/or physical attractiveness, you'll ultimately be attracted to the one with whom you can share a laugh or a cry. Sometimes this pull is so strong that it even overcomes other inequalities.

We're talking about the essence of an individual: their heart or soul. Some cultures specifically value this, as with the Sanskrit greeting of yogic practitioners which recognizes the meeting of two souls: "Namaste" meaning "The Divine in me bows to the Divine in you." The soul is the authentic self and it's a reflection of an individual's spiritual life. Hindus see each person as being a part of "God." Without a spiritual life, the authentic self struggles for expression because it must base its existence on its performance. A performance-based self must always be ready to perform or, harder yet, to repeat an earlier performance. This creates enormous pressure on the individual; the constant awareness that *who they are* is defined by *what they do or have done*. This translates into anxiety, a disorder that is rampant in our society.

As a psychotherapist, I have seen a disproportionate number of clients suffering from one form or another of anxiety. Our cultural values promote an adrenaline-based approach to life, with an emphasis on time-management in order to cram more into an already absurdly over-packed schedule. Even our children live by these schedules, racing from school to soccer practice, with no time for dinner and mom flying through the fast food take-out so the kids can eat in the car on the way there (and don't get me started on *what* they're eating!) A life lived at an unnatural pace is destined for some kind of physical consequences. In his book *Adrenaline and Stress*, Archibald Hart describes the effects of pushing ourselves through life in a fight-or-flight pace, elevating stress hormones on a day-to-day basis. These hormones were never intended by God or nature to be called into play except under dire circumstances, like running for your life from a spinosaurus, or fighting with a sabre-toothed tiger over your next meal.

A performance-based life leads to living in the fast lane, which takes its toll on the physical body. You can be sure that I'm talking to you if you've ever taken pride in your ability to "multi-task" – that's a recipe for stress, and stress creates free radical damage, the precursor of every degenerative condition or illness known. (We've already discussed that multi-tasking is actually ineffective; the brain simply can't sort out the multitude of tasks you assigned it to handle.) Another name for free radicals is oxidation, which is essentially what happens when metal rusts. Imagine your insides in a state of rusting – the damage is at first superficial, but if it continues unabated, it leads to real damage.

The first evidence of this degenerative process is signs of aging. The aging process is one of losses: greying hair (loss of color), loss of skin tone ("liver spots"), texture or elasticity, and loss of short-term memory. These are not conditions which we should naturally expect because of longevity, but are signs of the effects of stressors in our lives, like too little rest, too much caffeine or alcohol, a vitamin-poor diet, polluted air, and uncontrolled worry. The effects of the stress become new stressors that lead to increased anxiety, which becomes another stressor, and so forth. We must intervene at some point or else risk an incapacitating illness or premature demise. Too often we continue pushing ourselves, while justifying or rationalizing that we will slow down just as soon as _____ (fill in the blank with any of the following or your own: we pay off the car/house/credit cards/student loans; finish school/get the promotion/start the business/sell the business; the fish dies …). It's always about *tomorrow*, and tomorrow never comes! Every single day that I wake up, it's always *today!*

So far we've discussed the authentic self and the importance of depending on something more than a full calendar of activities to define our life and our *self*. We've also looked at the effects on our physical bodies when we neglect taking care of our needs, both spiritually and physically. Most of us know what our physical needs are. They include getting sufficient rest on a consistent basis, sleeping between seven to eight hours every night, eating a high fiber, wholesome diet that is as close to its natural state as possible (the fresher the better); and incorporating vitamins and antioxidants to combat the effects of our stressful lives and the pollutants in the air and food. We no longer get our nutrients from whole food sources so we need the additional supplements to help not only nourish our bodies but to help counter the toxins and free-radical activity.

In addition to diet and supplements, it is crucial to exercise to maintain a healthy weight and to elevate metabolism and strengthen the heart muscle, as well as to develop muscular strength and stamina. Studies have shown that we not only need exercise to improve our heart (cardio workouts) but weight training is vital for preventing bone loss. (If you don't like the idea of free weights, yoga builds strength from using the body's own weight.) If your bones cannot support the rest of you, you're in big trouble.

And finally, taking the time for quiet reflection or meditation— getting centered within and disconnecting from the sensory experiences that tax our psyches as well as our nerves is just as important as exercise. We need all of it to be truly balanced.

It's the centering of our lives that creates a sense of purpose and continuity to whatever we do. Recognizing the quiet space within is to honor that greater part of ourselves that is spiritual. We are spiritual beings having sensual and material experiences through inhabiting these physical bodies. It's not just a good idea to tend to our spiritual selves for the sake of feeling good and being less stressed, it's imperative that we reconnect our souls with the Source of life energy so that we can recharge. If we believe what the ancient sages and quantum physicists have agreed upon, that *everything begins as intelligent energy and then takes form according to thought*, then we can see the power of correct thought through connecting our mind to the greater Mind.

Prayer is one form of making this connection and can be seen as a conversation with Divine Intelligence. Since this Intelligence originates everything, then it might seem redundant to pray since every thought would already be known and anticipated before it was even prayed. The late Paramahansa Yogananda, renowned yogi, diplomat, and contemporary of Mahatma Gandhi, said that we are each One of His thoughts (God, or the Creator's). There must be a greater purpose to prayer and it may just be in the act itself. It may be that our seeking that which is greater than us is the answer. If everything that exists is essentially and fundamentally intelligent energy, then that would include us - *we are* intelligent energy. Even Christian Scripture agrees with this concept as we see in 1 Corinthians 3:16 where Paul says, "Know ye not that ye are the temple of God, and that the Spirit of God dwelleth in you?"

I like to think of myself as an extension of Divine Intelligence, operating on this physical plane with these physical limitations, but always having the cosmic power available to me whenever I seek it in solitude and silence. Meditation is the most direct route to experience this peace and power. It is the stillness of the senses that creates relief from constant stimulation. Eventually the mind becomes accustomed to the quiet and there is release from the continual barrage of thoughts. Even before that happens, there are imperceptible gaps between the thoughts when soul connects to Spirit and the circuit is complete. Self-help guru Deepak Chopra says that *these gaps* are the momentary periods when divine inspiration can come to us! In that moment, the body and soul can come away refreshed and renewed.

Just five minutes of meditation once a day can provide noticeable benefits. Twenty to thirty minutes allow time for the body to relax, thereby leading to a deeper experience. The benefits of twenty minutes of meditation practiced twice a day have been documented by researchers studying the positive effects of Transcendental Meditation on blood pressure, cholesterol levels and heart health. The study showed conclusively that there was a positive correlation between the practice of TM© and several physical benefits. Www.tm.org says the following about the physical benefits of practicing this type of meditation:

> Scientific research shows that the deep rest gained during the Transcendental Meditation technique allows the body to return to a more balanced state. It helps normalize high blood pressure, reduce high cholesterol levels, improve bronchial asthma, and provide relief from insomnia. It can even improve reaction time and athletic performance.

> People who practice the Transcendental Meditation technique say they have less stress, more energy, better sleep, and less tension in their life. Many find it easier to reduce alcohol use, stop smoking, and let go of unhealthy habits. Research also shows that they have lower medical costs, fewer doctor visits, and less hospitalization.

In some cases, it has also been shown to reduce the signs of aging, and may even appear to reverse them as well! It stands to reason that if we repair our cells and reduce the stresses in our lives, then the body will return to its healthiest state, sometimes better than we experienced in our younger years!

Such physical benefits, combined with the relaxing and refreshing rewards of meditation should be all that's needed to induce one to begin right away. But the reality of it is, that as badly as we may need something, for that very same reason we may never get around to doing it. We are too *busy* to meditate – I mean, who has that kind of time to just do *nothing* when there are endless tasks to get done? Sometimes the pace of life can be so intense that just trying to fall asleep at night requires some medication or alcohol. Therein lies the very reason that we really ought to create some discipline in our lives and take the time to do what is in our highest and best interest.

Everyone has the same 24 hours. What we do with that time is what makes the difference. If your life looks or feels even remotely like the description above, how are you planning on getting out of that cycle? What will have to happen for you to stop and take a good look at your life? How can you examine it for opportunities for growth and change?

Contemplation, reflection, and most especially, meditation, offer the high-speed connection to inspiration, imagination and intuition yet, ironically, it does so by forcing us to slow down. We are using our conscious mind to direct our attention towards our source, and it is through our subconscious mind that this connection is made. One useful computer analogy contrasts the power of these two aspects of mind by comparing the processing speed of the conscious mind at 2,000 bits of information per second, to that of the subconscious mind at four billion bits per second. That's two million times quicker and more powerful! While you are relaxing and refreshing yourself, you are simultaneously receiving into your subconscious mind the answers to the questions and concerns of your life, and the ideas to move you in the direction of your dreams and goals.

Everything begins as thought. Expectant thought grounded in joyful anticipation produces results. The image that you hold will come to you in form. Like attracts like. Your connection to Divine Intelligence will be felt in your heart as love and faith. Trust and confidence will be its expression through your personality – this is the real substance of self-image. As you experience this personally (it's not enough to just read about it, since it's much more than an intellectual idea) your reality will reflect your heightened level of awareness. Gratitude will be more than just an exercise, and will become an expression of your ever-increasing awareness.

Operating in the world with this level of understanding becomes an exercise in creative living. You move out of the realm of competition and into that of creativity. You no longer need to compete with another person, or with yourself. Your level of awareness dictates your results. You are a conduit or a channel, as Divine Intelligence flows in and through you, broadcasting creative energy throughout the universe. You are radiating joy, love and contentment, and ironically the desires that you chased before are now effortlessly attracted to you.

This is the authentic self in operation. This is the presence that attracts. Others want to be in the company of someone like this. Such presence connects with Spirit in others, and they experience feeling uplifted and even inspired. Your soul is the Spirit of God reflected through you and your smile reflects your soul. It elevates the souls of all those you encounter. Like-minded, like-hearted ones will be drawn to you, either to help you, or for you to help them and thereby receive for yourself the blessing of understanding that comes through giving.

On the most practical level, if your attention is focused on others and what you perceive that they most need in that moment, then their impression of you can only reflect that which they receive from you. To encounter sincerity and genuine regard coming from a total stranger is generally an unforgettable experience, as is that person. This is a gift we can easily give to another, but only when we have taken time to cultivate a relationship with our own authentic self. This creates a truly lasting impression.

CHAPTER 6

Who am I?

Okay, so who am *I* to be writing this book? A little voice inside me wants to say "nobody," - but I've had a book in me since I was in the fourth grade! I finally gave myself permission to live out one of my dreams and to write it, just like when I went surfing in Hawaii for the first time in my life at age 56. (If you've ever surfed in Waikiki, then you know it's *not* "the pipeline" and that most people *actually* live to see their pre-paid photos of themselves up on the wave.) Anyway, my venture into authorship while still in elementary school was short-lived but never forgotten.

I grew up commuting between Cleveland, Ohio and West Palm Beach, Florida for my entire childhood. Winter snows chased us south every December, but the lush beauty of summer in the Midwest drew us home again. A huge family on my mother's side provided lots of cousins to play with and created many great memories.

My parents were older when I was born – it was almost shameful for my mother to have had a baby at 35 years old (imagine the implications!). Not a big deal for my father – in fact, at 42, it would have been a point of pride. Now there's an example of the mindset of the 1950's, when our Victorian roots really showed up in puritanical attitudes, coupled with double standards for the genders. My only sibling was 13 years old when I came into the world, so she became like a second mom to me. That's relevant, because when I lost her to brain cancer when I was 40, my world collapsed and I was set onto another path.

The pattern of moving twice a year set up many significant paradigms that I still confront to this day. I know from personal experience that it really is all about perception, because it was not until I studied child psychology in graduate school that I learned the extent of that impact on my development! That's how it is with a paradigm – you don't know it's there until you try to go against it. Then you find yourself struggling against invisible forces which send you back to square one and you don't know why. I had repeated several patterns in my life throughout early adulthood and when I didn't repeat the pattern, I was just stuck – at a loss for what to do instead.

What got me un-stuck was the loss of my sister. Although we lived on opposite coasts, her absence from this world devastated me and caused the beginning of a *transformative melt-down*. There was a long time when I thought I would never laugh or be happy ever again. It hurt to breathe. Just getting through each day was all I could do. The death of my dear sister was my greatest pain, but during a period of about eighteen months I suffered multiple losses. In that same week I also lost my aunt. My husband and I separated, both our dogs died, and we lost our home; two friends were killed, and another died of AIDS; my mother-in-law died; I was divorced; and I lost my father one year to the week of my sister's death.

I would never be the same again. But that's how life is. There is a line in the movie *Out of Africa*, in which Meryl Streep's character is narrating from England after returning home ill and broken. She says, "This was not how I thought my life would turn out." That was exactly how I felt. We all do that - we anticipate the future according to some idea that we nurture and then believe. A well-rehearsed thought is actually what makes a belief. We think the same idea over and over again until ultimately it assumes the status of a belief. I had always believed that my sister and I would have each other into old age, two little old ladies growing old together. We had talked about it many times.

So many things that I had believed about the future were now clearly not true nor would they ever be. I began an intensely introspective period of therapy, while studying to become a marriage and family therapist. Both processes required deep examination of my life and soul, and for the first year I cried more than I talked with my therapist. Little by little, I began to feel alive again. I started looking towards the future. Although I had been going to school and working for the airlines, I had been on auto-pilot. Eventually, as I developed a connection with life again, I began to see how the events had re-shaped me and created a new depth in my character and in my soul. I developed empathy to such a degree that at times my clients have thought I was psychic, and it's quite possible. Well-developed intuition is a *knowing* feeling that comes of its own accord, but develops out of a sense of rapport and an understanding that we all are fundamentally the same. Any real differences between us are external; on the inside, we are all equipped with the same emotions and feelings, mixed in varying proportions according to our life's experiences.

Surviving these fires of life has brought compassion to the work I have done and hope to my clients. It is deeply rewarding work to participate with another person as they journey through their own pain and fear and to be able to be there when they break through their conditioned thinking into freedom. To witness the "Aha!" moment is truly an honor.

It has always felt like a privilege to be allowed into the inner sanctum of another person, especially a client who is virtually a stranger who comes in with their pain and opens up with their willingness to be vulnerable. I have honored that trust that has been extended to me in the client-therapist relationship, all the while marveling at the beauty of the process. I know that some clients have told me things that they've never told another person, or perhaps never admitted even to themselves.

The best part of being a therapist has been the personal growth that I've had the opportunity to experience. Every time I speak to a client, *I* am also listening. Every time they speak, I learn about the resilience of the soul. When I witness the changes within another person, it's a testimony to the human spirit, and I grow, too. Every client has taught me something about myself and about life.

Mental health and wellness go hand-in-hand. I can recall treating a young woman, a mother of five children and a full-time employee, who was suffering from outbursts of anger and anxiety and for which her doctor had medicated her. I regret to admit that we had been working together for close to a year before I learned that her diet consisted daily of cola for breakfast, nothing for lunch, and typically two candy bars during the afternoon. Her problems were at their worst when she got home from work and had to deal with kids, husband, dinner, homework and baths. This lesson taught me to inquire about eating habits, caffeine and sugar consumption, and to look for general signs of nutritional deficiencies and not to assume anything.

Around this time I began studying the importance of getting sufficient nutrients and eating wholesome natural foods, as well as the impact of high-glycemic foods on blood sugar levels and weight. There's a lot of evidence supporting the relationship between a healthy body and a healthy mind; studies have shown dramatic improvements in severe cases of mood and cognitive disorders when nutrition has been specifically supplemented.

Our society has become accustomed to medicating itself for every unpleasant feeling. We have been conditioned to believe that there's a quick fix for almost every aspect of human nature that we find disagreeable or uncomfortable. Most prescribed medications carry the potential for side effects or residual conditions; many cause new conditions requiring additional medications to be prescribed. One woman came to me complaining of feeling disoriented and disconnected from herself. She had a history of treatment with over 25 different medications and her condition continued to worsen. Working together and with the help of a naturopathic psychiatrist, she discontinued most of them while adding specific herbs and vitamins, and we worked through the underlying issues that had led her to seek help in the first place. There have been many other examples of significant and dramatic results from the combination of addressing both body and mind.

I have always pursued personal growth and development. Studying astrology and doing birth charts were my first experiences "counseling" others. I began studying Eastern philosophy and religion during my early 20's, exploring such writers as Maurice Bucke, author of *Cosmic Consciousness.* In my later 20's I became involved with est™. During my 30's decade, I was deeply involved with the Christian church. Later I began studying the Indian system of yoga, the science of religion. Paramahansa Yogananda's *Autobiography of a Yogi* bridges East and West, yoga and Christianity, and the interested reader is invited to refer to the Recommended Reading List at the back of this book. Until his death a few years ago, I was an avid student of Dr. David Hawkins, psychiatrist and author of numerous books on consciousness and enlightenment, most notably *Power vs. Force.*

The study of the human mind and nature of man leads a therapist in humanistic and spiritual directions. Always in search of deeper understanding, the study becomes one of the self, and of Self. As personal understanding increases, so does the understanding of others, since we are more similar than not.

I was one of millions of viewers worldwide who was impacted by Rhonda Byrne's film, *The Secret,* a phenomenon that spread globally through word-of-mouth. The message of the docudrama style movie was the power of our thoughts and the effects of the Law of Attraction. "Like attracts like" is the essence of the Law, which is always at work regardless of our awareness or attention to it. If we don't operate with the Law in mind, then our life becomes one of default, delivering to us what we've unwittingly attracted through the thoughts and feelings to which we've given our attention. The film was a series of messages delivered by numerous coaches and consultants who are successful in the personal development field, and illustrated with dramatic or comedic vignettes. The primary narrator and host was Bob Proctor, an individual who has created phenomenal results in his personal life and in the many thousands - more likely millions - of lives that he's impacted over his 40-year career teaching people how to get the results they desire in their lives.

The impact of the movie created the next shift in my life and my career turned in the direction of personal development. This was not a big turn, given that my work with clients had already moved into that arena. Wayne Dyer's *Power of Intention*, with its quote from quantum physicist Max Plank, "Change the way you look at things and the things you look at change," caused the first shift in my thinking for over 20 years. Later I knew I had much to learn from Bob when in the movie he stated that we each have enough electricity in our own bodies - 11 million kilowatts per pound of body weight - to supply the power to illuminate the entire North American continent! After studying with him, I became a LifeSuccess Consultant™ presenting life-changing information, teaching people how the mind works and their own capacity for achieving their dreams.

Despite my background, I felt an old limiting belief (those ugly paradigms!) trying to stop my progress and movement into something new and exciting and for which I was born to do. Yes, even therapists get stuck when they want to change (Spoiler alert: Bad joke ahead ..... Q: *How many therapists does it take to change a light bulb?* A: *Only one, but the light bulb has to really* want *to change.*) I really wanted to change, but I needed that personal support in order for me to get un-stuck. That is where the role of a coach or mentor comes in, and with that support I was able to move into what was new territory for me. I have been able to see myself from the perspective of another who can see me objectively, as well as having already done it themself.

This fit in with my life focus on wellness and fitness, working out harder in my 50's than at any other time in my life. Working with my personal trainer brought me to an all-time low body fat level, but more importantly, to a new sense of confidence and eagerness to try new things – like surfing in Hawaii, and participating in the Camp Pendleton 10k Mud Run – running Suicide Hill – two miles *uphill*, climbing five foot walls and crawling through 30 feet of mud to the finish line!

You can't out-perform your self-image as it is right now. I have worked to develop my own image until it resonated with what I wanted to project. This is a life-long process because growth is stimulated by our continuing desires for more new experiences. No longer am I content to put anything off until later. "The time is *now!*" is my mantra.

What about you? How long has your book been inside you? What are *you* waiting for?

CHAPTER 7

Creating Your Image

People-watching is a popular armchair sport in which you can safely view plenty of action without risking personal injury. It's a pastime for a lot of people who prefer to remain in their comfort zone. Those who aren't content with sitting on the sidelines of life put themselves onto the playing field. It's a small percentage of people in life who are willing to take the risks and get onto the field.

Assuming that you are one of that small percentage, what image will you portray to the world? Are you ready now to be out on the field? Once you're in the game, you must be ready because the time for practice is over. Running a 10k when you've prepared for several weeks is a very different experience from when you haven't practiced at all and have gone out and just muscled through it. I know, because I've done it both ways. If you don't want to suffer, then it makes sense to build up your strength first. In fact, that's why so many people don't run races or do some of the other things in life that require preparation and sweat – it's uncomfortable, if not downright painful.

This lack of preparation stops people from pursuing their dreams. Our mental muscles need practice and preparation as much as do our physical muscles. In the same way that our muscles develop from consistent exercise that pushes us past our comfort zone (no pain, no gain), our ability to think bigger thoughts requires us to stretch our thinking a little every day, gradually adding more and more weight to those thoughts. There are possibilities that can only occur to an individual if they have been exposed to other new relevant ideas that serve as a foundation. This way of thinking is not new. In the 19th Century, German poet and philosopher Johann Wolfgang Goethe wrote about making a decision and he said:

Until one is committed,
there is hesitancy,
the chance to draw back,
always ineffectiveness.
Concerning all acts of initiative
there is one elementary truth,
the ignorance of which kills
countless ideas and endless plans:
That the moment one definitely commits oneself,
then providence moves, too.
All sorts of things occur to help one
that would never otherwise have occurred.
A whole stream of events issues from the decision,
raising in one's favor all manner of
unforeseen incidents and meetings and
material assistance which no man
could have dreamed would come his way.
Whatever you can do or
dream you can, begin it!
Boldness has genius, power,
and magic in it.

When I began my weight training program, I wasn't ready to make many concessions in my eating or lifestyle. After six months, I followed my trainer to a new gym with kickboxing classes – something I had always wanted to do but had never felt fit enough to try it. This took my training to the next level. A few months into kickboxing, we used a metabolic test that revealed a low rate of calorie burning and this propelled me to begin looking at my food intake in a new and more disciplined way. I couldn't have done that nine months earlier, but I had grown into the mindset by my on-going exposure to new information and my willingness to move out of my comfort zone. This led to the most dramatic results I had ever achieved – my all-time best weight and muscle-to-fat ratio. Years later, those results remain because my mindset evolved.

The greatest thing about those results was the effect they had on my attitude and my confidence level in all areas of my life. I had confronted a paradigm that had been denying me the body I had desired to have all my adult life. "You're too old ... your body type is wrong ... you'll get hurt before you get there ... this is too much work ... you don't have time for this ..." It just wouldn't shut up – not until it was apparent that I had *made a decision.*

In *Think and Grow Rich,* Napoleon Hill talks about the power of this simple act of making a decision and its ability to overcome formidable opponents and obstacles. He says simply, "Success requires no apologies. Failure permits no alibis."

The image that you want to create is already within you. It only needs encouragement and nurturing to express itself – *your* self. Who is it that you admire in your life? The answer to that will provide great clues as to what qualities you find desirable. There may be specific qualities that you appreciate in different individuals. The reverse of this is also true. There may be someone towards whom you feel an aversion; often this indicates that you share similar *shadow* qualities with that person and it creates a repelling force. Opposites attract and you can use that information to consciously develop within yourself those qualities you appreciate.

An effective tool for developing positive qualities is the use of affirmations. Write out those qualities and read them aloud at least twice a day, first thing in the morning and just before bed so that they will be impressed upon your subconscious mind when it's most receptive. It's most important that you feel into the emotions of the statements because this is where the power of affirmations lies. The statement should reflect the first person, and be in the present tense. An example for creating a more positive response when under stress might sound something like, "I am relaxed and patient in all circumstances." Notice that it only states the desired behavior or attitude and assumes it under all conditions. Recording your affirmations and listening to your own voice repeating them has an especially deep effect on the subconscious mind. There are also many pre-recorded versions available to purchase that are equally effective.

The creation of a dream board is another effective way to condition your subconscious mind to see yourself differently and in the new way. Look for pictures of people who present as if they possess that quality or thing that you want for yourself or are in places or situations that you would like to visit or experience. If the picture speaks to you, then it's resonating with your innermost feelings. Cut these out and put them onto a large board that can be mounted where you will see it daily. Include on this board words and phrases that reflect messages that you want delivered to your inner self. Most importantly, include photos of yourself on the board among all the pictures. When you look at the board, you will identify with the photos of yourself and automatically include the surrounding images in your identification. There are many ways to have fun with dream boards and it is a great bonding exercise for couples and families. Children naturally know how to dream and you will be amazed at the conversation that will emerge during the crafting of a family dream or sharing your dreams with your loved ones. Furthermore, this is a powerful way for you to create desirable paradigms in the minds of your children.

Simplistic as these exercises may appear, don't underestimate their power to influence the very impressionable subconscious mind and to create real and lasting change. The conditioning that runs our life was impressed upon our mind over time and has been reinforced by our continually "obeying" it. It is only through repetition that it has become the strong directing force that it has become. Through the repetition of new desirable thoughts we can over-write the script and create a new conditioning, a re-conditioned mind.

When I ask clients what it is they want, often what I hear is what they *don't* want. Sometimes that's all we know for sure; we're certain of what we've had that we don't want anymore. If that's the case with you, then use that list of what you don't want to identify what you do want. For example, if you don't want to be overweight anymore, then state what you do want - to be healthy or athletic. Then write that down. If you don't want to be timid any longer, write down that you are confident and easily express yourself in all situations. These affirmations will begin to manifest as qualities that you will possess as a result of changes in your behavior that reflect your new beliefs. Thinking differently and feeling differently will lead to different behavior and actions. Within a short amount of time, considering how long you've been functioning in the old way, you will begin to see results – you'll notice a difference in yourself. This will inspire more change and growth, until one day you will realize that who you are has evolved into the person you had once only dreamed of being.

As you are ridding yourself of things you don't want, be sure to get rid of them in your surroundings. If you have a problem with clutter and want to be more organized, go through your closets and physically remove the clutter from your home and office. Clean out the corners and release some of the physical items that you no longer want and repeat your affirmations while doing so. It can be quite therapeutic to pick one closet per week to unload. As we let go of some of the junk we've stored, we also then create room in our lives for the things we *do want*. Energetically, your de-cluttered surroundings will positively affect your inner environment, creating more space for the new you.

Recognizing yourself as a spiritual being will be an advantage because the change that you desire begins in the field of the Divine Intelligence. If you seek Divine assistance to develop qualities that serve the greater number, you will receive all the help that you need. When I learned to ask for help for myself *in order to benefit others*, it was almost like the genie in the lamp answering my wishes. That wasn't where I started, though. My history of fruitless attempts finally led me to realize that when I took my eyes off myself, then I ended up getting what I wanted in the first place. At first it seemed that I was getting something different because the "how" didn't look like what I thought it should. The beauty of this is that your personal achievement is a small glory compared to the joy in being used for a purpose higher than your own.

How will you know if you've successfully recreated your image? You'll know you were successful when you no longer concern yourself about your image. When your self-consciousness disappears then you have become unattached to the superficial concerns that have driven you for so long. That's when your core values are directing the course of your life. Your focus is on others and being of service in your own unique way, using your special gifts and talents.

What does this feel like? One feeling is freedom! You are free from second-guessing your words and actions. Your self-expression and creativity flow. Ideas come to you fluidly and the ones you give attention to seem to effortlessly attract whatever is needed for their manifestation. Everything seems possible and yet you have learned to identify what is worthy of your time and attention before you can effectively focus your energy. You become more selective and more effective. Goals become related to a cause because you see yourself as connected to the rest of the world. This leads you to recognize another feeling: gratitude. Your understanding that you are part of something greater is a humbling experience; this leads naturally to gratitude.

Of all the beautiful qualities one might aspire to possess, an attitude of gratitude is the most attractive, as it reflects the purest heart. And gratitude, like the other emotions we've discussed becomes part of our personalities when we practice it daily. Express your gratitude at the end of every day by looking for at least five things for which you're grateful and write these down in your journal. This will foster your attitude of gratitude, especially as you heighten your awareness of all that is flowing to you. Your faith in the Law of Attraction will expand and your ability to attract will become even more refined.

CHAPTER 8

You're Known by the Company You Keep

Earlier I mentioned the saying that goes, "Who you will be tomorrow is dictated by the books you read and the people you associate with today." Our circles of influence are so powerful and yet we seldom stop to consider their importance. Did you know that it's possible to determine the level of someone's income by looking at the incomes of their closest friends? It's rare to see someone making $25,000 a year hanging out with millionaires. This makes sense on a practical level because people with similar resources can afford to live in the same neighborhoods and play at the same level in life.

You may be thinking that sounds unfair because the individuals wanting to advance in life could end up stuck at their current level like in a caste system. It brings to mind the idea of needing work experience to get a job – so how do we ever get that first job? We get it, as most all of us have, through a determination to become employed. It's a dominating thought in our minds until we have achieved it. Then not only do we have a job, but we have also attained job *experience*.

So how does this apply to the individual seeking to increase their income and to advance in life? If you're not where you want to be right now, then hanging out with other people who think like you do won't provide the pull or the inspiration to move out of your comfort zone. Now this isn't a suggestion to throw away all your lifelong friendships, especially because this is a generalization – you may have a relationship that stimulates and inspires you and yet you're both at the same place in life. Or you may have that rare friend who sees *you* as the mentor to get them to where you are and who isn't bringing you down but inspiring you, as well. We can be teachers and students at the same time. But generally speaking, we are drawn to others with whom we feel comfortable and who reflect our basic outlook on life. Remember, the comfort zone is where things are familiar and conform to the conditioning and paradigms of your life – your habits.

It's understood in the tennis world that if you want to improve your game you need to play with people whose skills are better than yours. This causes you to stretch your skills. Of course, it may not be easy to convince them that you're going to be able to keep up or be a strong enough opponent to make it worth their while. But if you love the game and you sincerely desire to improve, your passion and enthusiasm will convince them. Just like when you convinced your first employer to hire you.

Human nature draws us to comfort and security. We're not comfortable associating with people who have accomplished more than we have. This is a common occurrence for people when they're dating. We're most comfortable dating others who are "at the same place in life." We measure ourselves against their success and if we fall short in our own assessment of ourselves, then we become intimidated by that person. Very few people care to subject themselves to such internal judgments and so the tendency is to avoid those situations. But if we treated it like a tennis game and we sought out the strongest players in life, we would find ourselves being stretched and strengthened. And confidence would be born out of our experience.

Intimidation is a nice word for fear. Fear of *what*? Fear of what *we think* another person *might* think of us. I place the emphasis on it being about our thoughts, and not of any quantifiable external object; I also emphasize "*might*" to draw attention to the *uncertainty* of it. In the process of dreading judgment by another, we are fearful of their rejection. Our fear is that they may discover that we're not as good as what we'd like them to believe. They may find out that we don't even think we're that great. And so we blame them and say, "They are intimidating" or "unfriendly, arrogant, egotistical, materialistic, or greedy."

When we are honest with ourself, we realize that this is about *us*. It is within *our own minds*. The entire experience has been an internal one, originating from a perception. Unless you have consciously and consistently examined your reactions in life, it's unlikely that you actually respond to the events at hand. It's far more likely that you automatically react according to your lifetime of conditioning, to your perceptions. Your world-view is your perception. The glass is either half empty or it's half full. Einstein said, "The first thing every individual has to decide is whether the universe is a friendly or unfriendly place."

Once that orientation is established, everything that follows must align with that point-of-view, which acts like a filter for your mind. Your perceptions are your interpretations of life events that pass through that filter. You literally create your own reality. Not only do you create through the quantum process as your thoughts manifest into form out of the zero point field, but also on a more fundamental level, through your interpretation of events. We create our reality or life situations by our thoughts about the things we've interpreted through the filter in our mind. It may not be true or an accurate perception but you created a reality based on it!

The people we choose to surround ourselves with will reflect our orientation. If we see the universe as unfriendly, then we'll seek out people who "make us feel safe." Of course, no one "makes us" feel *anything*. We do that all by ourselves. The very fact of the existence of that figure of speech tells us how conditioned we've all been by the idea that other people or things outside of ourselves somehow dictate how we feel. WE are the ones having internal dialogues, telling ourselves and even telling others such things as, "You make me so mad." "He made me feel stupid." We may go so far as to accuse others of being responsible for our behavior! "I wouldn't have done this if you hadn't done that." It's pretty easy to spot when some highly dysfunctional person does this, like the alcoholic accusing his partner of driving him to drink because of their nagging [of course they're nagging – they live with an alcoholic!]. But many high functioning people have also developed the habit of talking this way about their feelings and it ultimately leads to them believing the words they're speaking. There's a huge difference between the feelings in the following two statements; try reading each one aloud and see for yourself: "You make me so mad." "I feel mad when you do that." One is enraging; the other is empowering.

We must assume complete responsibility for every feeling we have. There are no exceptions to this rule. This might possibly be one of the greatest failings of our society at this or any point in our history. As a group, we have abandoned our grandparents' values in which individual accountability was a respected and revered quality of character. In their time, the issue of self-esteem was virtually unheard of, while the concept of self-respect was paramount and derived from integrity and morality. We have dubbed them "the Greatest Generation" for their persevering work ethic during the World Wars, and their enduring commitments to both their country and their marriages. The Sixties saw the decline of value being placed on both of those commitments. The Vietnam War and the subsequent loss of confidence in government and large corporations made suspect all the values of that generation. This was reflected throughout our culture, as the sexual revolution was underwritten by new discoveries in birth control, and chronicled in music with songs like *Love the One You're With*. Sex, drugs and rock 'n roll became the new church for many of America's 76 million Baby Boomers.

My perspective on this subject was up close and personal. Never radical or militant on any issue, nonetheless I participated in some demonstrations and festivals, and looked the part enough to have caused my parents several years of disappointment and sleepless nights. I lived through what I'm talking about and I believe that the moral decline created a decline in morale. There was general loss of direction among so many of us and a loss of faith in what had been taken for granted by so many generations before us. Politically there was a lot of finger pointing between the "Make love, not war" group and the powers-that-be. Maybe this was when the blame-game got its foothold in America – never before in this country had the "establishment" been challenged by youngsters, and they felt no need to explain or acknowledge the opposing point-of-view. I might have found it scary if I hadn't been in the middle of it, but that's a matter of perception, isn't it?

Our national consciousness has taken quite a ride from the days of throwing off the King's dominion over us, all the way to suing a fast food corporation because their hot coffee was just that ... too hot. That event has impacted me as one of the greatest examples of failure to assume personal responsibility in even the most mundane situations. *It's not my fault,* and *get rich quick* are phrases that ring out here and they describe *entitlement*: a privilege or a person's right to receive something. If everyone were to operate that way, then life would become a battleground, either in the courts or worse. Dog-eat-dog would be the prevailing rule, and there would be chaos.

I'll get down off the soapbox and quit preaching! But there is a point to be made here. Our willingness to take personal responsibility for everything in our life, including our feelings, is an empowering attitude that leads to success. Think about a time when you heard of a lawsuit filed that allowed the plaintiff to avoid personal responsibility while seeking a huge settlement. What effect did that have on you? We cannot entertain feelings of victimization and feelings of empowerment at the same time, so we must choose one.

Who we associate with will influence our choices and decisions. Healthy and supportive relationships always draw the best out in both people. You should be able to share your innermost dreams with someone close to you and know that you will receive encouragement, support and affirmations of your ability to accomplish it. There should be no competition between you, neither in accomplishments nor for attention. If the people in your inner circle thrive on the drama in their life or in yours, then you know that you are associating with people who see themselves as victims. In some instances, they may have been actual victims of abuse or assault; this discussion is not meant to describe them, unless they have come to that point where their identity has become wrapped up in what has happened to them and to the exclusion of any other input, such as therapy. I'm talking about people who love to discuss the latest incident in which they were disrespected, insulted, mistreated, neglected, or wronged according to their perspective. Their story takes on more importance than the possibility of resolving the problem. Any attempts on your part to offer advice or suggest a solution is generally met with well-defended explanations of how that would never work and that this is "different." In other words, they are not truly seeking a solution or any resolution, but rather are getting their feelings of significance from your sympathetic interest and continued attention. Exhausted is probably how you feel after spending a certain amount of time with these people. I refer to the people who practice this behavior as "emotional black holes" because they suck you in but never get filled up – and once you can't offer anything more, you are discarded for the next sympathetic ear. The exhaustion you feel may be physical, but I'm actually referring to a kind of spiritual drain on your soul. I also have another name for them – "psychic vampires," because it feels as if they are draining you of your life force.

You cannot afford to expose yourself to these kinds of people. Unfortunately, they're sometimes right within our own family and that poses a more difficult, but not insurmountable problem. The method for dealing with them is called *setting boundaries*. That means you define for them (first for yourself) where you begin and they leave off. In other words, you draw a line defining your personal psychological space that they learn they can't cross if they want to spend time with you. Your objective is not to change their personality but to require them to behave in a particular manner with *you*. The way that you do this is by modeling for them what you consider to be appropriate topics of conversation and by what you pay attention to when they're talking. Your attention is the key because when they lose your attention then they are not being reinforced in their behavior. Change the subject when it's negative, pessimistic or critical. You are not required to listen to everything someone is saying; interrupt it with a complete topic change, or, if you're confident enough to be direct, simply state that you'd rather not discuss this topic, and then move on to something positive or neutral. If you do this, there will be some people who will fade out of your life. They are disqualifying themselves from being in your inner circle. Let them go, wish them well in your heart and send them a card on their birthday.

Many of the relationships that survive despite the changes in you and the relationship will be with people who are genuinely concerned with your best interests. We are all at different stages of our development and we are here to help one another. As you grow, they will too. In fact, you can measure your own progress by the behavior of those around you. Interestingly, once you arrive here, you will suddenly notice that all the people in your life contribute in some way to your growth and provide opportunities for you to contribute to them.

Once you begin to see yourself as someone who makes a contribution to others then you will see others for those same qualities. As you look into others' hearts, their external accomplishments become secondary to who they really are on the inside. This allows you to be discerning in your choice of friends, and also levels the playing field in terms of professional achievements. When your relationships are grounded in being and not in doing, then the energy generated is conducive to growth for both of you. It's better and more meaningful to have one deep connected relationship than one hundred superficial acquaintances. If you believe that we truly are here to help each other, then understand that the people you attract and who attract you are the ones with whom you share a mutual energetic frequency.

You will experience this frequency as a feeling within yourself. Recalling the earlier discussion regarding feelings leading to behaviors, which lead to results, you can see the importance of aligning with others who value and share your outlook on life. Why would you want to spend time with anyone who doesn't? The world is full of wonderful people, many who would love to be in your company and who see life much as you do or have something to offer you in your growth. Make up your mind to attract these people to yourself. Create an affirmation such as, "I magnetically attract to myself like-minded, like-hearted people." Write it out and read it aloud several times daily until you have it memorized, then continue to speak it even when you see it manifesting in your life.

Visualize the kinds of people you'd like to have in your life. See them from the inside out, and imagine how your life will be when these people form your personal inner circle. You might want to go so far as to create a dream board where you put pictures you find in magazines or photos of friends and family who you feel are like-minded and like-hearted. Use text on your dream board to tell your subconscious mind when you look at it how you want to feel and think. "Excited, fun, sharing, joyful, happy, active" are just a few of the words that might describe how you'd like to program your subconscious mind. Put on your board pictures of people enjoying life — vacationing, socializing, whatever resonates with you. Remember, you're creating a new paradigm and conditioning yourself to behave in a new and different way. The sky's the limit — allow yourself to soar!

CHAPTER 9

Re-Programming Your Self

Before my son was born, my husband and I both expected to have a daughter. We had never discussed it with each other, so it was a surprise when we learned that our baby was going to be a boy. It didn't take long to fall in love with the idea of having a son (about a day!), but that experience really stuck with me. We weren't even aware of our expectations of a girl until it was contrasted with a different reality.

This is how we learn what our expectations (and our paradigms) are in life – by the contrast of a frustration, disappointment, or even a surprise. We each have so many bits of data that have been downloaded into our minds since the moment of our birth, and most of it lies hidden in the recesses of our subconscious mind. It's an amazing process if you stop to imagine how that stored information is stimulated by a relevant situation that triggers the utilization of that data. Even more amazing is our ability to process the contrast between what we currently want and what's stored. This is truly the miraculous part – our ability to think, rationalize, and to make choices.

The stored data represent our conditioning, the paradigms that dictate how we respond to life's situations. It is an accumulation of all the information that has been organized into "standard operating procedures," or rules for survival. All this is kept in the repository of the subconscious mind and it is there for one purpose only and that is to maintain the safety and survival of the human being. Notice I didn't say anything about expressing our talents, maximizing our opportunities or evolving spiritually. That is not the job of the subconscious; it's too busy maintaining the physical body and keeping the heart beating, the respiration going and all the hormonal and enzymatic processes working while we're busy doing other things, thinking or sleeping.

If paradigms dictate our automatic choices, then we could say that we are *programmed* by them. When we're functioning on automatic and not consciously thinking through what our response will be in any given situation, then our programming will produce a predictable outcome.

That's a starting point for discovering what constitutes our programming: what outcomes do we continually get? When you notice a pattern in your life, then you have a choice to break it. Maybe you always end up in similar job situations or you find that you continually attract the same kind of friends or partners. That reflects a pattern in your functioning (it's not "bad luck"! — Hopefully by now you're recognizing that you make your *own* luck). The pattern stems from your programming in that area of your life.

This is where the fun starts. This is the path of self-discovery. It's a lifelong path. You will always have more to explore as you grow into a greater and deeper self, but it gets easier as you become acquainted with the terrain. It's through living life to the fullest that you will be able to determine where you get stuck. It does require pushing out of the comfort zone and up against the terror barrier of change before you'll discover what the sticking point is.

The Terror Barrier

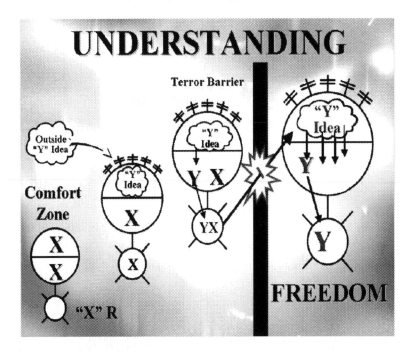

The Terror Barrier is that wall that we hit when we're trying to stretch outside our normal zone of comfort and do something out of our ordinary experience. Think of each of your ordinary thoughts and feelings as "X" and see the congruence between what you think about and what you feel. As long as you continue to stay with familiar X thoughts and feelings, you feel in harmony and comfortable. As soon as you introduce a new idea or a "Y" thought, however, then disharmony or dissonance arises. For example, let's say that you've been at your current job for five years and you now decide that you want to change jobs. The idea of changing jobs is a "Y" idea. This "Y" idea is loaded with emotion – excitement for change, anticipation of advancement and greater opportunities, eagerness for increased income, and a host of other emotions. All ideas that pass from our conscious mind into our subconscious mind do so because they have emotions attached to them, so this new "Y" idea is moving down into the subconscious mind.

Here is where it gets sticky because the "Y" does not resonate with all of the stored "X's." Your subconscious mind begins to deliver up to the conscious mind recollections of similar past experiences when you encountered frustration or maybe even failure, fueling thoughts of doubt about your ability to do the new job or feelings of dread over the interview process, resulting in worry and anxiety. Soon, your experience becomes dominated by these negative thoughts and feelings, as more and more of these "X" files are opened and presented for your consideration…and obsession! As the anxiety grows, it takes on a physical aspect and you experience fear in your body – and this is where you get stopped. The closer you get to the point of contact with the new idea, such as going on the interview, the greater the fear becomes until it grows into overwhelming fear, or terror! This is the Terror Barrier, because that terror can stop us from pursuing our dreams. We hit that wall and too often, we turn around and go back. We return to the point where we started and then rationalize why we could go no further. Many in our inner circle who are comfortable with us continuing to occupy the same box with them will sympathize with us and tell us that we're better off without that job. When we change our own lives for the better, those around us have two choices; to revel in our success, or confront the "Y" in their own lives. It is why we often lose friends when we move forward in life.

The problem is that when we return to the point where we started, we're not the same person. We've now internalized a *failure*, because that's what a decision to quit is. In fact, quitting is the only kind of failure there is – refusal to persist and instead, giving up on the dream. That failure is now a part of our programming. It will lower our confidence the next time we consider going after another job. It becomes another "X" in the stored files.

Now imagine a different scenario. See yourself noticing the worry and anxiety, but this time you say to yourself, "Oh, look at that! I must be moving out of my comfort zone because look at what's coming up!" Your level of awareness has grown to the point where it *expects* to confront old conditioning and paradigms and is ready for it. The thoughts and feelings may even escalate into an experience of fear because you have not been down this road before and fear of the unknown is a common and expectable experience. The fear does not escalate into *terror*, however, because you understand what's happening. You continue on your course and you move into and through the unknown – and you come out the other side! Whether or not you get the job is not the point, because now you have something much greater and that is the experience of going after what you wanted. This is confidence building and it becomes your *new* "X." In other words, you have re-conditioned your mind to include a bigger view of the world and of yourself.

The next time you encounter another "Y" you will have the benefit of this experience. You will better know what to expect and you will understand the process that your mind goes through every time. *Your results are dictated by your level of awareness.* As your level of awareness rises your results will expand and so will your satisfaction and joy.

One of the ways that we can begin to raise our level of awareness is by identifying what may be limiting our thinking. Explore your known belief systems: religious, philosophical, cultural, racial, and gender-based; examine what you believe to be true in each of those systems. We have all received so many messages throughout our lives. The older the message, the deeper it resides within. Just think of everything you heard and were told about God, the world, other people, your family, intelligence, abilities, personality or the future. Oftentimes the message is sandwiched into a more palatable ideal, such as to always be giving and to put others before yourself - that you should not want anything for yourself because that is selfishness. This is a powerful message to overcome because it confronts a core belief that you are selfish if you don't accept it. This atmosphere of doubting the integrity of the questioner creates blind obedience in the faithful, and that leads to forgetting the questions.

The internal conflict is enormous for those who do question values for themselves. The pressure of conforming to the group is one of the strongest, most basic needs in man, according to Abraham Maslow in his "Hierarchy of Needs".

> Maslow posited a hierarchy of human needs based on two groupings: deficiency needs and growth needs. Within the deficiency needs, each lower need must be met before moving to the next higher level. Once each of these needs has been satisfied, if at some future time a deficiency is detected, the individual will act to remove the deficiency. The first four levels are:
>
> 1) Physiological: hunger, thirst, bodily comforts, etc.;
> 2) Safety/security: out of danger;
> 3) Belongingness and Love: affiliate with others, be accepted;
> 4) Esteem: to achieve, be competent, gain approval and recognition.

Maslow's Hierarchy of Needs

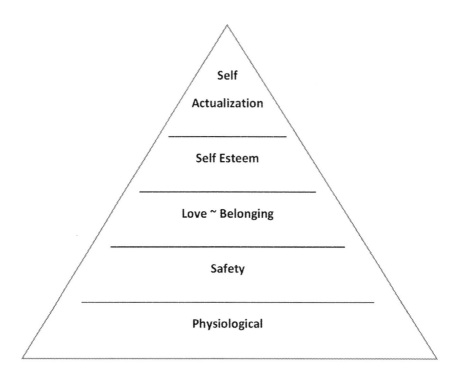

Self
Actualization

Self Esteem

Love ~ Belonging

Safety

Physiological

Our self-esteem and self worth are derived from our self-image, which comes from our earliest environment. If we're told things which conflict with our innermost voice and our innate *knowing*, then we must either sacrifice our security by going against the group and suffer their efforts to correct us; or sacrifice our connection with Spirit and our own internal knowing and lose our confidence in our ability to discern for ourselves. Most of this goes on at a time in a child's life when they are still processing subconsciously, so without a filter their ability to evaluate is not yet developed. This information then is stored out of sight and forms the conditioning or programming. Their sacrifice is unconscious and invisible to them, although it may be experienced as a loss of joy or spontaneity.

So what were *you* told? How did you feel about it then? How do you feel about it now?

Ask yourself, "Is that the *truth*, or is it just what I *believe*?" There is a distinction here. We tend to believe whatever thought that we have rehearsed, or others have repeated to us enough times; suddenly it assumes the status of a belief. Our mind likes to take shortcuts. We generalize in order to be efficient in our thinking and functioning. We have to generalize in order to categorize and then be able to arrive at a conclusion. If it's furry and it purrs, it's a cat. We could not function for long if we had to figure that out every time we encountered a furry, purring thing. That's what we do on all levels. We generalize and then we categorize, and then we label it and we're done. This is great for meeting up with unfamiliar cats, but not so good when we're trying to grow mentally, emotionally or spiritually.

The second way we raise our level of awareness is through an encounter with the paradigm itself. This occurs when we step out into the unknown in pursuit of something we desire. I believe it's important to have the motivation of the desire, otherwise when the discomfort begins there will be little to keep us in the pursuit. We can use the well-known "pros and cons" list to begin drawing out what thoughts and feelings we're having. When done with full attention and intention to gather data, it will cause ideas to emerge, much like pulling a very long chain up out of a very deep well – one link connecting to the next, going ever deeper. This is the one time when it's okay to write down every limiting thought you have about yourself or your idea; this will go on the con side. It's critically important to know what you're up against internally. Repeat the process for the pro side, finding every positive thought or feeling you have about yourself and your idea. Some of these will be so good that you'll want to create an "affirmation card" using them to read every day. This will help to re-condition your subconscious mind.

As long as we're alive, we're going to confront our programming. Even when you feel you've grown, you will find yourself continually outgrowing earlier thoughts and beliefs - even newly developed ones that may serve you for a while but will eventually be replaced as you continue to grow. This process of the expansion of our souls is what life is all about. The *real* truth resides with God, the Source of everything. Our purpose, ultimately, is to move ever closer to that Truth. Our *original* programming resides within us, as one ancient motivational book states ...*the Kingdom of Heaven is within*. As you come to know this on a personal level, you will realize that you have been given everything you need to live a joyful life.

CHAPTER 10
What We Think About We Bring About

"Fear of the unknown" is an all-too familiar expression acknowledging that most of us become at least a little bit anxious when faced with the unknown. Touching again on our most fundamental needs, Maslow's "Hierarchy of Needs" mentioned in Chapter 8, places safety and security on the second rung of importance. What that means is that it's human nature to seek security and to place it high among our priorities in life. It's right up there with food and shelter, a need that's basic to the human race. This is why the majority of people do not experiment too much with their lives.

What is considered the norm is getting an education, marrying and having a family, beginning a vocation or profession, retiring, traveling, and dying. Particularly in America, the vast majority of us fall into this pattern of life, but with wildly varying outcomes and degrees of success.

Among those in our society who do deviate from what is the normal course in life, there are essentially two groups. The first group is made up of those who want to make their mark on the world and so they devote an extraordinary amount of time to the pursuit of knowledge and the development of certain skills, to the exclusion of the other "normal" activities that defines most people's lives. The second group is made up of those who feel that life is an adventure and they want to play, explore the world (externally or internally), experiment with athletic or artistic endeavors, and generally "find themselves." There may be a third group, those who start out in any one of the groups but then default to substance abuse and possibly homelessness; but they are outside the scope of this discussion.

This chapter is written for anyone who is living the normal life but who dreams of being in one of the other two groups. Especially if breaking out of the normal life evokes feelings of fear and confusion, then this chapter will provide a blueprint for making that escape. There is no greater waste than having a life and living it unfulfilled. Wayne Dyer says, "Don't die with your song unsung." Stories abound of people who have overcome incredible odds against them, and they serve as role models for everyone else. Pioneers in thought, word and action, these people changed the world by being faithful to their inner vision.

I tell my worrying, anxious and depressed clients "Don't drive through life looking in the rearview mirror." Every single thing that distresses you is either in your past or in your future – which is NOWHERE because neither one of those is a place at all. They exist only in your mind. If you were to take the word "nowhere" and break up the syllables differently, you'll see it can also read "now here." When we are HERE NOW, it's not possible to be stressed, worried, fearful, sad or anything other than content. When we are fully present in the moment and consciously aware of our self and our surroundings, peace is the first thing we notice.

Stop right after reading this instruction and set this book down, closing your eyes and taking a long, deep breath in through your nose, then releasing slowly out your mouth. Focus on the sounds around you, the smells, the temperature and the feel of the air on your skin, how your body feels in the chair you're sitting in; opening your eyes, focus on what you can see around you right now. Just check in with your body and your environment, and focus on staying in touch with this moment, taking another cleansing breath or two.

What's the first thing you notice? Everything quiets down, doesn't it? The stress we feel is inside of us, it's our mind working overtime. As soon as you pull the plug on all that noise, it suddenly becomes peaceful. You can put this to the test by doing this exercise anywhere – find a noisy spot and try it. You'll be surprised to discover that you have the power to control your inner experience. I'm not recommending doing all your meditating at the airport or an amusement park, because it is most effective when you find a spot where you can be undisturbed and allow yourself to fully relax. And yes, that *was* a meditation, however brief it was. Now the longer you sit in meditation, the more "noise" you'll have to contend with when the mind starts trying to insert thoughts. And your mind likes to be busy! This is natural and your only job is to notice the thought and return your attention to your awareness of the present moment – the sounds, your breathing, or a mantra. There are many ways to meditate and it's a personal preference which technique you'll find most natural for you.

Meditation will have the effect of quieting your mind even during the waking times of your day. You'll find yourself feeling calmer, more even-tempered, softer and kinder. There are physiological benefits from meditating and there are numerous studies available to learn about those benefits. The most dramatic evidence will be your own experience of the soothing effects it will have on your psyche. One client of mine who had suffered from panic attacks and high generalized anxiety, found dramatic relief from just five minutes of meditation every morning coupled with affirmations. She was able to discontinue her anti-anxiety medication – she actually realized one day that she hadn't refilled it for almost two months, and she still had nearly a full prescription left. This is powerful! When she took my suggestion and added another five minutes, she began having more profound insights into her own behavior and motivations and those of others. My usual recommendation is to add five minutes at a time until the time is at least 20 minutes. This allows the mind time to settle down and to engage at a deeper level.

One phenomenal benefit of meditation that relates to breaking through fear and out of old paradigms is the ability to control one's attention. This ability is enhanced through continued meditation, but even after the first few times, this ability emerges prominently. The process of meditation, in which it's necessary to direct the attention away from intrusive thoughts, trains the mind to do this at any other time. This leads to the realization that we have thoughts, but that we are not our thoughts. This makes meditation priceless, if you'll pardon the worn-out cliché.

When negative thoughts surface while contemplating your dreams and goals, the ability to shift attention away from those thoughts is the key to achieving those goals. *Where attention goes, energy flows.* Our understanding of quantum physics informs us that it is through our thoughts that energy takes form. It suggests that the creative power of the mind is such that any idea or thought is an energetic pulse that has the potential to manifest itself into like form. The *observer effect* states that when waves of energy (potentiality) are observed by a human (consciousness), it collapses into particles (matter). If human consciousness impacts this field of potentiality, then our expectations form the basis of what manifests. "Like attracts like" is the rule; this is the essence of the Law of Attraction and it's based on energetic vibrational frequencies. If those frequencies are a match, then the attraction is in place and it's only a matter of time before it manifests physically.

The Law of Gender states that there is a season for the gestation of the seeds of everything in the universe, from blades of grass to ideas. There was a time when mankind didn't understand how babies were created; the period of gestation was too long to make the connection, given their level of awareness. Today we don't have the level of awareness to understand how long it takes for an idea to germinate. But just as in the planting of seeds of grass, we must have faith that our idea is growing and allow the time needed to complete its cycle. We must nurture the idea, keep the soil of our mind well fertilized, and water it with love and attention, all the while having faith that it is growing - especially when we cannot see it. We do not dig up the seed to examine it for signs of growth. We should not dissect the seeds of our dreams, either, and risk ripping out the roots that have sprouted beneath the surface.

One of the most powerful tools for cultivating our ideas is Goal Setting. Research has shown:

A classic study on resolutions found that 60 percent of people who set a goal give up on it within 3 months. But that means 40 percent succeed. The difference between the ones who reach their goals and those who fall short? Successful changers seek out or stumble onto the right strategies.

But in order to know and remember your goals daily, it is imperative to write them down! The two fundamental laws of the universe have to do with *order* and *movement*. Goal setting creates order out of the energy of thought, giving it form and direction. In *Think and Grow Rich,* Napoleon Hill focuses on the necessity of writing out your goal in detail, including what contribution or service you'll be providing others. It's also imperative that you put an end date on it to create a sense of urgency and to create movement. Finally, it must be read out loud every morning and night, and ideally, at least one other time during the day. So you will want to put it on a card that can be carried with you; you might want a second one on your nightstand by your bed.

Bob Proctor taught me to write out my goal statement beginning with, "I am so happy and grateful now that ..." The rest of the sentence must be in first person and present tense. This is critically important because otherwise you'll be training your subconscious to *wait* for the goal instead of appreciating it *now,* as if you already have it. Let's say you want to lose 30 pounds and that would put you at 140 pounds, and you'd like to do it by December first. Your goal statement might read something like this: *I am so happy and grateful now that I weigh 140 pounds or less by December 1ˢᵗ or sooner.* Always allow for something better than what you're imagining by including the qualifying statements such as: *or sooner, or better, or more.* If losing the weight has an added benefit for others then be sure to include that in the statement, such as: *I feel so good now that I have more energy to play with my children.*

In the beginning, when reading your goal statement, you may feel dishonest or disbelieving of what you've written for yourself. That's perfectly normal and part of the process. If you have written a big enough goal, yet one that you can still imagine achieving, then you will feel the stretch. You should feel both excited and nervous at the prospect of achieving it. With time, you'll become more comfortable reading it and hearing the words, until eventually you'll be inspired every time you hear yourself read it.

Visualizing your words as you read them is an important part of directing energy towards the goal. See yourself doing and being what the statement is saying; feel the emotions as you mentally rehearse the scene. The goal statement is not a magic wand; the words alone have no power other than that which you bring to them. There is magic in the process of aligning your dream, your thoughts, your feelings and your expectations. You'll find that your faith in yourself in achieving this goal will begin to grow as you continue in this way.

Create a "vision board" or "dream board" to help stimulate the emotional part of you. Find pictures that appeal to you and cut them out and put them on a large poster board; fill it up with photos of you, pictures of places you want to go, words and sayings that inspire you, and ads of items you'd like to have. Make it colorful and fun; continue to add to it as you go along. Expand your inner world by hanging your "dream board" where you can look at it often and expose your subconscious to the images and the feelings they evoke. This will help transform your goal into a burning desire.

Thought is the most powerful form of energy in the universe. If thoughts do become things, then wouldn't you want to choose the good ones? Take control of what you allow to enter your mind – don't let negative friends, radio or television pollute your precious *gold mind!* Think positive, creative, expansive thoughts. You have nothing to lose and everything to gain.

There is no stopping anyone who is driven by a burning desire and is backed by faith!

CHAPTER 11

You Can't Teach an Old Dog New Tricks... or Can You?

So how old is *too* old? Who decides? If you worry that you are too old, then that reveals that *you believe* you are too old. The saying goes that "today's 50 year-old was yesterday's 30 year-old." In other words, not only are people living longer lives and producing more throughout their lives, but they look better, too!

There are lots of ways to fight aging. Cosmetic surgery, tummy tucks, hair dye, facials, cosmetics and anti-aging skin creams are just a few. These are all really good things and it's important for us to feel our best and especially to feel young and virile, because youth is associated with virility and power. But at the same time, we should gracefully accept the stage that we are in. What's more, we should embrace that in arriving at this place we bring along all the learning accumulated over our lifetime.

In Eckhart Tolle's book *A New Earth: Awakening to Your Life's Purpose*, he talks about how our ego's identification with the body, whether negative or positive, has a profound effect on our mental and emotional image of our self, as well as our health. He says: "If you don't equate the body with who you are, when beauty fades, vigor diminishes or the body becomes incapacitated, this will not affect your sense of worth or identity in any way." I contend that it takes a mature individual to really accept and *feel* this. Mr. Tolle goes on to say: "Body awareness [i.e. recognizing that your worth is not determined by the state of the external body] not only anchors you in the present moment, it is a doorway out of the prison that is the ego. It also strengthens the immune system and the body's ability to heal itself." In other words, looking inward and knowing that we are so much more than just that external manifestation of a mature body demonstrates wisdom. We should revel that we've accumulated knowledge and wisdom that we would not have otherwise gained if we were still the age that we are trying to look.

I started my career as a therapist at 45, which is a little after the curve for most professions. But in this particular field, age is considered a benefit because it's understood that you *have* gathered life experience and wisdom along the way. In general, however, we do have a societal bias about being "over-the-hill." Meaning that you've passed your peak and have lost your usefulness and value to society. Who wants to hear from somebody who's old? What could you possibly know about what's going on in the world - what's trending or the latest meme? If you buy into that belief, then it becomes true for you. If you allow yourself to think that your value has diminished, or if you look at other people your age and feel that they're secondary or past their prime, then it becomes true for you. Even when we marvel at people who've accomplished great things in their 70s and 80s, it reveals a prejudice - however subtle - that we don't expect people to be productive throughout their entire lives.

What does it even mean to be old? What *is* old? One definition states that the word "old" is a synonym for "aged." And a definition of "aged" is "showing evidence of advanced erosion." Well, I reject that one! However, a definition that I found that I *like* is: "Stored for a period of time in order to produce the best flavor." I think that is a much more desirable, accurate definition.

Aging is readily apparent in the human body but is it really just all about how a person looks? Or are there other qualities to being mature or advanced in years that cause people to become fearful of becoming old themselves? Don't we actually fear becoming useless or dependent on someone and making no contribution to society? What about the fear of getting sick and the associated vulnerability? It isn't just old age that scares us, but the idea of helplessness and the possible ensuing hopelessness. It is one of the most basic fears that people have throughout life. Because our society is so fast-paced, always moving in the fast lane, we find it hard to imagine that we can still be productive, feel gratified and experience a satisfying life while living at a much slower pace.

As a society, we are so consumer-oriented and materialistic that we're geared (programmed) toward production. If you aren't producing, then your value is diminished. There may be some truth to that when we look at the elderly in nursing homes, or those in the "golden years," especially those who do not have the financial resources to travel and do all the things they dreamed they would at retirement. There is a tendency to think that a life like that looks boring. On the surface it does look boring, even desolate, when you consider a life without purpose, dreams or goals.

We all need goals. The fact that we've arrived at a certain age doesn't eliminate that need. In fact, it may be more important than ever at that time of life to have a dream or goal. Where is it that you want to go? In what way do you want to grow? What is it that you want to produce or create once you're no longer under pressure to support a family, struggling to make a living and trying to just make ends meet? Unfortunately, it's easy for most of us to go through our entire adulthood without having any goals and not even notice. If your parents didn't teach you to have dreams and goals, then it's not going to be a part of your programming.

Most of us are so busy between jobs and careers, family responsibilities of children as we run them back and forth to soccer practice and juggle homework projects all while attempting to keep up with managing the house. So many people that I talk to ask, "How will I ever get all of this done?" Garages need to be cleaned, and grass keeps growing. The suggestion that one should have a goal is like adding another thing to their To-Do List. Most people don't want to add one more thing to their list – they're looking for ways to shorten that list.

So if we've never had the experience of setting goals, then learning that new skill becomes like "teaching an old dog new tricks." The importance of goals is that they create order in our life, which is then followed by movement, and these have been called the first two laws of the Universe. Order is naturally followed by movement. Develop a plan and it will carry you in the direction of your stated objective.

What if you're already retired? What if you feel that you're already past those "productive" years? Is it possible to make goals and develop that order and momentum at such a late stage? Yes, not only is it possible but it might even offer the greatest level of satisfaction.

You must be willing, however, to let go of old habits. Especially the habits that don't support your stated goal. Habits are a reflection of our conditioning or our paradigms. How do we break out of our paradigms? Dr. David Hawkins refers to a "paradigm of allegiance" in which he describes one particular paradigm: it is the presumption that our perceptions of the world that we experience accurately represent *reality*. We do what Dr. Hawkins describes as "seeking comfort and mental reinforcement by congregating with others who share the same reality or paradigm." There's a little hint to breaking out of that paradigm right there. We can start by associating with people who DON'T share our point of view about life and the world. Of course, that's not what we typically do. We gravitate to those who are like-minded and share our outlook on the world. It is comforting to know that others believe as you do.

But what if you don't feel, on the deepest level, that this is all that life has to offer? What if you question the path that you've been on throughout your life? Is it better to ignore those feelings, deny them, or pretend that they don't exist? Doing so can create a mental flatness, and even a spiritual deadness. It results in a lack of aliveness or connection with all the possibilities that life has to offer.

The beginning of a remedy for this would be to find others who can introduce you to new ideas and new concepts. Your ego, which always likes to be in a position of authority, may seriously protest. The older we get the less we like to feel ignorant, so our reaction can include intensely critical, judgmental thoughts and possible feelings of anxiety, even fear. That's the ego talking... protesting! The truth is that this place is the single most beneficial state to be in when you want to grow. Admit to yourself that you *don't* know and that you want to *grow*.

I recall the day that I was driving to the graduation ceremony for my Master's Degree. At 44 years old, I felt a tremendous sense of accomplishment. On the radio was the story of a 94 year-old woman who was on her way to her graduation ceremony for her bachelor's degree. I imagined the sense of accomplishment that *she* was experiencing that day – her satisfaction at the culmination of all of her hard work. Overcoming all the obstacles - getting to class, doing the work - just parking in the university parking lot must have been an incredible hurdle for her (always was for me)! Imagine all the objections she must have endured from caring relatives when she announced that she was going back to school. But she knew something very valuable. She was the sole experiencer of her own life. No one else was going to take her place in experiencing her life. If her life was going to be what she wanted, then she was going to have to make it so.

You might be thinking to yourself, "Where in the world did that woman get the energy to do that? She drew on the strength that was within her. Motivational speaker, Denis Waitley, has stated: "...Goals provide the energy source that powers our lives. One of the best ways we get the most from the energy that we have is to focus it. That is what goals can do for us. Concentrate our energy."

A lot of people complain and say, "I'll be 35 years old when I finish school." Yet, that 94 year-old woman knew that she was going to be at least 94 before she finished school and she didn't allow that to be an excuse or a reason not to persevere. She knew that how she spent the time allocated to her in this life was her own responsibility. She believed in the saying "If it is to be, it is up to me."

Ask yourself what you are going to be doing one year from now … five years from now? Think back five years ago – did you plan then to be where you are now? Did you *have* a plan for now? It doesn't matter what you *didn't do* – as long as you use that to propel you into action *now*. All that matters is what you do right now. Now is where life is being lived. Not tomorrow. Not yesterday. When you get to tomorrow, it will still be "today". Life takes place in the present moment. All the rest of it is in our minds.

If you find yourself thinking too much about the past, it can be depressing. Conversely, worrying about the future is the stuff of anxiety. Make a deal with yourself: let thoughts about the past or future be directed towards creating a new goal. Don't allow yourself to expend your energy and waste precious moments of your life thinking about things that are not here. Those memories are just neuronal pathways.

At some point I realized that when I die all of my thoughts and memories will go with me. If I want immortality, then it must come through my creating something lasting – a legacy - a contribution to my community and to the world. If I don't contribute then I'm just taking up space. Maybe that sounds harsh, but this contribution doesn't need to be a cure for a disease or an ultimate solution to a global problem. It could be initiating a recycling program in your neighborhood. It could be holding drug-addicted babies at the local hospital, who need that tenderness and care as they begin their journey in this life already saddled with issues most of us cannot comprehend. Or it could just be taking the extra time, despite your busy day, to listen to your elderly neighbor speak about something important to them. These are worthwhile contributions. Every single thing that we can do to help just one person will affect the consciousness of the planet. Quantum theory says that we're all entangled and each a part of the whole.

We don't live in a vacuum. We are all interrelated. The very breath you exhale expels electrons from your body into the atmosphere, which are inhaled by another person, which then contributes to the life processes of their body. Then they exhale those atoms and electrons that go on to be breathed by the next person. We're all connected or entangled. It is difficult to see because we are all housed in separate bodies and equipped with egos that want to be unique - separate and special.

If you find it difficult to imagine creating a goal for yourself at this time in your life, ask yourself, "Who can I help? *How* can I help?" Take an assessment of your talents and skills. Write them down, then begin to imagine how any one of them might help others. How can those talents make a difference in someone else's life? Don't worry if you get stuck – this may be new territory. Just stick with it until you have a list that you feel good about.

When we give, that creates space in our own life and attracts to us what we're wanting. Test it yourself. Think of something you could do that would benefit another person or group. Spend some time contemplating this. See what happens. You will begin to notice an influx of energy and ideas. You'll start feeling more inspired. The universe will support your efforts as you take your eyes off yourself and seek to help someone else.

I'll close this chapter with a wonderful example of an inspired thought. Mahatma Gandhi of India encouraged his followers to "be the change you want to see in the world." He was able to influence 200 million people of his homeland to come together in unison. Gandhi led a non-violent protest that took 17 years and which eventually overcame the rule of the United Kingdom, the greatest military power on earth at that time. He accomplished this with just a thought, an idea – something he envisioned which had the power to create that result. Obviously, he used his faith to the greatest degree imaginable. Then he waited, expectantly, for that which he knew would *have* to come to pass - that his vision would manifest in the physical realm.

Allow Gandhi's example to inspire you and set you into motion. Remember, "Imagination is more powerful than knowledge." Use your imagination. Don't dismiss any thought or idea that comes to mind just because it came from *you*. Any idea that comes to you does so because *you have the power to make it come to pass.* Otherwise you wouldn't have the idea in the first place. You are the channel.

I believe the reason that I haven't been inspired with the cure for cancer is because it's not among my talents and skills to bring that into physical reality. But I also know that the gifts and talents that I have are *mine*. They're my responsibility and I have an obligation to use those to my greatest ability in this life.

If you are still reading this, then it's speaking to you. Don't believe that it's too late. Use this time to do something now. Just don't keep waiting.

CHAPTER 12

What's Missing in this Picture?

The physical world reflects your internal world. As you look out at the world, it's like looking through the windows in your house. When they're dirty, all you can see is the dirt on the windows. Everything outside of the house seems clouded by that film of dirt. When they're clean the world seems to sparkle. You look outside through those clean windows and you see possibilities. The light shines through. You see the beauty that's out there.

It's much the same with our perceptions. Our perception of the world is actually a reflection of the inner world where we really live. How can we hope to see the beauty outside of us if we can't see it within us? We'll have difficulty recognizing it even if we're looking right at it. At the risk of sounding too esoteric, there really is no "out there." It is actually a projection of the reality within us. All that we observe comes through the filter of our perceptions. It's entirely a subjective process and yet, so often we'll point to our observation (through the filter of our interpretation of events) and use it as evidence to support our point of view. This is known as "circular thinking." As the name implies, you end up back where you started. Furthermore, you usually convince no one but yourself. One way to break the circular thinking pattern is to begin to look at what your assumptions are on any topic.

Since this book is about you and your image, let's start there. Take a look at yourself and ask yourself this: Do you like what you see? Focus on your good points. What are your strengths? Be specific and write them down. Then focus on your shortcomings. Find the habits that are in need of change. Start there. Identify the most glaring ones. And let that be your starting point. Then get feedback from someone you trust.

Oftentimes our perception of ourselves is far from what others see in us.

Take a survey of those people closest to you asking them what is your greatest strength and what area needs work? Make sure that these people are specific with you. You're looking for the general consensus among your friends. You need this information in order to proceed to the next level. Make sure the information is from people you trust and whose opinions you value and who also have your respect. Their lives must in some way be something you admire. Now, put together this information that you've gathered from your trusted sources and compare that with what you've gathered for yourself. Look for commonalities. What do your sources agree upon regarding your strengths and what needs work. This is also a good place to stop and look at how close your self-assessment is to the feedback you received. Is it close? Or are you needlessly hard on yourself? Or maybe you don't expect enough from yourself? Perhaps you recognize that the observations made by your friends are accurate, yet you feel they lack the understanding of why you operate in that manner or what your motivations are. It will be at this juncture that you have a decision to make. You will have to decide if you are going to continue going in the same direction or if you will take this feedback and use it as a mirror, in order to redirect your path. If you find yourself wanting to explain yourself to your friends on the areas that need work, then maybe you've fallen into the habit of making excuses, both to yourself and others.

Can you identify one glaring habit in need of change? That will be a place to start in your process of initiating change.

Because we understand the Law of Attraction, our focus needs to be on that which we desire, not on that which we don't want. Using the identified habit as a point of reference, ask yourself, "What is the opposite of that habit? How would I be functioning without that habit?" Get a picture in your mind of what that would look like in all its details. For example, if running behind schedule is one of your flaws that you would like to correct, then imagine what your life would be like if you were to arrive everywhere at least five to ten minutes early. Visualize what it would be like to arrive early. Notice the feelings that you have. Notice the mental state that you're in. What else would it affect? Would you behave differently? What would your attitude be like? How would others respond to you? How do you feel about others' responses to you? In this way you're giving energy to that which you desire. *Where your attention goes your energy flows.* This would be a good time to create some affirmations around this topic. Be specific and paint a word picture that you can feel as you read those affirmations daily to reinforce the programming in your subconscious, as you recondition your mind. It might read something like: "I feel happy and relaxed as I arrive at my appointment ahead of time and ready to take care of business." Words have power and energy, and as you say those words aloud over and over, day after day, you are reprogramming and reconditioning your subconscious mind. *Your subconscious mind does not know the difference between fantasy and fact.* Whatever is delivered and impressed upon it will be received and stored as truth.

It *is* within our ability to change the programming that resides within us. It does require attention and effort though, but it is well worth it. You may be thinking, "What difference does it make if I change one habit? We're talking about a new image - a new persona - how can one habit make that big of a difference?"

There's an example that I'd like to share with you that came from one of my art teachers when I was studying photography. He pointed out to us that if we took a black and white photo that we had printed from the dark room, there are always bits of lint on the filter or the lens and each speck of lint creates a nearly imperceptible dot of white in the dark areas of the image. He had us see the difference for ourselves by printing two copies of the same photo. One photo we retouched with the inks made specifically for the black and white photographs with a tiny brush – so tiny that it only had a few bristles. With this tiny brush we would dot out each one of the nearly invisible white marks. Although we could not see those white marks in the un-retouched photos without a magnifier, when we compared the two photos side-by-side the retouched one was unmistakably the preferred version of the two. In every instance, the retouched photo will be picked by the observer who won't know why. It's because the small things make a huge difference. We may not be able to identify exactly what detail is different, but we know *contextually* that the one that has received the extra measure of attention and love is better. This illustrates that much of what we observe through our eyes is interpreted by our mind, unrelated to our vision. It also illustrates the concept of the "Razor's Edge" – *that the line that separates winning from losing is as fine as a razor's edge.*

J.C. Penny was 91 years old when interviewed and was asked, "How's your eyesight?" He replied, "My eyesight may be failing me, but my vision has never been better."

Your ability to visualize yourself as the person you want to be is a creative process. We are the creators of our own reality. How would you like to be perceived? What would you like people to think of you? Who is it you want to be? Paint a picture of yourself. Fill it in with details. All the small things count. Remember the example of the photo. You can tap into the reservoir of Spirit and through your intuition discover the self you want to be. Remember that Intuition is one of the six intellectual faculties that Napoleon Hill talked about, and Wayne Dyer asserts that it is how God speaks to us. Make the time in your life to seek and to *listen*. Pray about it. Contemplate and meditate. This is important. The most important work that you do for your self will be done from the inside. When the inspiration comes your imagination will kick in. The ideas and the pictures will be there. Be sure to write them down. Don't delay. Timing is very important especially when it comes to inspiration. If you allow too much time to pass before you record your inspired ideas, it's likely that you'll lose them. Inspiration is like little gems or nuggets, but these precious pieces can easily be lost.

Capture the inspiration on paper and use it as the topic of your contemplation and meditation. Allow it to grow. Don't try to direct it, just feed it with your attention and positive expectations. Maintain an attitude of curiosity, and see your life as one in which the possibilities and the potential are infinite. Your potential *is* infinite.

You are a spiritual being in a physical form and gifted with an intellect. This intellect allows you to be like a receiving station for the ideas and the intuition that come through us from Spirit. We human beings are portals in the quantum universe.

Allow yourself to be used by Spirit. Ask to be shown what you're missing or what you're not currently seeing. Then confidently wait and **expect an answer**. Psalm 27:14 reads: "Wait for the Lord. Be strong and take heart and wait for the Lord."

CHAPTER 13

Fake it till You Make it

At first glance that may appear to read as if I am instructing you to be a phony or not authentic. But in fact, I want you to discover the hidden parts of yourself that exist within you. Each and every one of us has all the qualities that we need to show up as the person we want to be. However, we don't always utilize those qualities or traits. There is nothing we need to get from outside of ourselves. EVERYTHING we need is *already* within us. Everything *you* need is within *you*. You possess all the resources that you're ever going to need. It's only a matter of excavating those resources and bringing them to the surface. Once you identify a quality that seems to be lacking, you can begin to practice and rehearse it until it becomes a natural part of who you are.

When I was in the eighth grade I was a very unhappy and depressed young girl. My family moved a lot and I continually felt disconnected from my peers and the rest of my world. It appeared that they all enjoyed a life that I didn't have access to. As I sat in class one day looking around me at the kids who were obviously having fun talking with each other and laughing, it suddenly dawned on me that I needed to change the way I operated. I was tired of feeling sad and lonely and I thought to myself, "What if I just pretended to have a good time?" On some intuitive level I thought that maybe I'd feel better and maybe it might cause people to want to be around me. I just followed my intuition. I did it. In fact, I did it immediately sitting right then and there. I just made a decision. That's what it is. It's a decision, and in my case it was just to *act* happy and to *appear to be* happy. It had an almost instantaneous effect on my life. Right there in that classroom, on that very day, my life changed as I discovered that as I acted happy, I was projecting happiness and this was attracting people to me. They seemed to be drawn to me like a magnet. Suddenly people were smiling back at me and they were including me in their conversation. I found myself *experiencing* the life I'd only been observing up until just a few minutes earlier.

Dramatic changes followed very quickly after that. I found myself going from literally feeling like "a nobody" to dating the captain of the football team. That might seem like a superficial value, but for a teenager it's very important to have that sense of belonging. I'm sure that the inspiration for what I did came from my own misery and loneliness. I know for certain it was an inspired idea (inspired = in spirit). And it's one that has impacted me my whole life. I've shared that story with many clients, especially ones who were depressed and unable to see how they were ever going to be happy again.

Our feelings and attitudes actually register in a field of consciousness at a certain level that can be measured and calibrated. Dr. David Hawkins speaks about this in his book *Power Versus Force*. He says, "The higher feelings like love and gratitude all register higher in terms of their vibration, and they're also associated with a higher level of consciousness." These feelings tend to cluster at a particular level in terms of fields of consciousness. In other words, all the energy that is out there in the universe is not just all mixed together like a big pot of soup, but it exists in certain levels in which "like attracts like." That's why when we find ourselves in a particular mood, we attract more of the same to ourselves. So by faking a feeling you get in touch with the feeling and you connect with that field from which the feeling comes, and it feeds more of the same to you. Wayne Dyer described a study in which individuals performed an act of kindness and then experienced an increase in their serotonin levels; this effect was also experienced by those who only were a witness to an act of kindness between two others.

Let's look at this on a more practical level. Faking is really pretending. Kids do it all the time and we see the value of it for them. We know that they're exercising their imagination and creativity. We know they're practicing certain life skills that they'll need in the future. They rehearse being a doctor, teacher or parent, playing-out their imaginary roles. We can do the same thing. We can practice and rehearse a role until we're called upon to perform it. This is something you can easily do starting right now, right where you're sitting. For example, the next time you don't feel like smiling, smile anyway and see what happens. Although not everyone will respond to you with a smile, most will, and you'll find yourself feeling differently. (This is really a pretty safe experiment since mirror neurons will support you in being mirrored!) It will engage different hormones in your body and set up a different vibration in you.

The smiles you'll get in return will be self-reinforcing and create a positive feedback loop, which will encourage you to smile more often until, finally, there is no pretending involved. It has become a natural self-perpetuating behavior.

Another area in which practicing a new way of being can have a dramatic effect is in acting brave despite being afraid. First, develop the resource of getting centered through breathing. Learn to take a few deep breaths that you hold for several seconds before slowly exhaling; feel the grounding effect in your lower belly or womb space as you visualize it filling with this centering energy; notice how much more present you're feeling in your body. Then, look for an opportunity to exercise bravery by putting yourself in a situation where you know you'll feel intimidated. Take a few of those centering breaths - then step into the situation and stay present in your body, breathing consciously as needed. This is courage. *Courage is bravery in the face of fear.* Notice how the dread of it was so much worse than the actual experience of being there, and might even seem a little silly afterwards. Savor the feeling of your accomplishment and take some time to journal about it.

Practice the skills that you want to become second nature in your personality. I'm suggesting that you look for opportunities to put yourself in an uncomfortable situation. You do this intentionally with the idea that you'll be able to rehearse the skill that you want to become a natural part of your being. If you know that patience is not one of your strengths, then find the longest line at the market and put yourself at the end of it. Whatever you would normally do in that situation would be an expression of your typical behavior; determine what is the exact opposite of that behavior and do that. For example, if you usually become abrupt or impatient with other people, then deliberately set out to be friendly to the people in line with you, interact with the cashier when you get to the front of the line, and generally force yourself to behave in a way that's opposite to how you normally act. This is a creative process and requires some imagination. Because it is a creative process, which originates with Spirit, it draws to you the energy and the inspiration necessary to accomplish it.

If this is sounding to you a lot like acting, you're right. Take an acting class to practice assuming roles. You'll be given scripts in which you can immerse yourself in a character and begin to become acquainted with the process of assuming a different persona. The process is the same if you're attempting to modify your own character or personality. Although this may sound artificial or contrived, it's still necessary to do something different if you want to get a different result. You cannot continue to do the same things and expect to get a different result. (That's the definition of insanity.)

There is a model of energy psychology called "Tapping." This is a technique that utilizes the energy meridians within the body in much the same way that acupuncture and acupressure do. Certain points on the body respond to stimulation, particularly when applied concurrently with a specific statement. Tapping has been known to alleviate physical pain and even the effects of traumatic memories, as well as aid in the cessation of smoking and other habits and phobias.

The Tapping Map

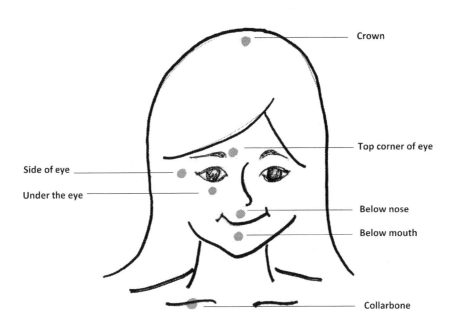

1. Begin with identifying the desired outcome. Assess the degree of distress [0 = none; 10 = greatest imaginable].
2. This becomes formulated into a statement, coupled with a positive regard for oneself. For example: "Even though I have this headache, I still deeply love and respect myself."

3. Using one or more fingers of one hand, tap the "karate chop" edge of your other hand, while repeating the statement aloud three times.

4. Stating only the problem ("this headache") begin tapping each of the points on the map 7 times while repeating the statement aloud.

5. Re-assess the level of distress [0 – 10].

6. Repeat for any remaining distress. State: "Still have this headache" or "Still hurting." Continue until distress is at 0.

This is an extremely effective yet simple approach to many problems. Applying it first to aches and pains increases your confidence with the technique as you see the immediate results. Then use it for anything you can think of that you would like to see changed!

There are some other practical techniques you can use in which you can create a new awareness of yourself. Remember, what you're doing is reconditioning your subconscious mind. Your own behavior is one of the strongest ways to do that. Your behavior stems from your feelings and your feelings come from your thoughts. The thoughts that you give any time and attention to with any degree of emotion move from your conscious mind and become impressed upon your subconscious mind. That's why the power of a dream board is so great. It creates cells of recognition for what you want in your life and delivers them to your subconscious mind, the directing center for all your actions. Cut out pictures from magazines and put them on your dream/ visualization board. Use pictures of things you want to be, do and have. See yourself being and doing and having those things. Put a picture of your face on a car that you want to drive or a body you want to have. Use words that resonate with you and paste them all over the board. Use words that describe how you want to be. This is all imprinting your subconscious mind. Remember your subconscious mind does not know the difference between fact or fiction, reality or fantasy. It all goes in evenly and is impressed upon it. It is not the job of the subconscious mind to determine what is true or not true. The subconscious mind is only concerned with your survival.

Create affirmations, or positive statements about how you want to be and feel, telling yourself what you need to hear. An example of an affirmation on patience might sound something like: "I am patient, kind and understanding under all circumstances." Write your affirmation on a card and read it out loud several times a day everyday, until it eventually becomes part of who you are.

Write out another affirmation as if you're speaking to yourself and use your name in the affirmation. Include the qualities and acknowledgements that you would like to hear. You could even give it to a close friend and ask them to read it to you every day. Be sure that when they do that you allow yourself to receive it and let it in. You may be objecting right now to what may seem contrived or like false flattery. But, did you know that flattery is the only form of lying that we universally find acceptable and even desirable? Remember the goal is to recondition the mind. Just play with some of the suggestions given here. Observe for yourself the effect on your attitude and your interaction with others. As you are tapping in to the higher vibrational fields you are going to experience an elevation of your own feelings and your own vibrational level. Remember your feelings are a reflection of your vibrational levels. Feelings are your physical experience of your own vibrational frequency. By tapping into a higher vibrational frequency, it elevates your own frequency. It becomes easier and easier to function at that higher level.

What starts out as pretending becomes real. The idea that you are pretending is really just to trick your ego. You are the very same person who is behaving in a different manner. Regardless of whether you call it pretending or a change of behavior, the ultimate goal is to get the desired change. Agreed?

The ego is likely to put up quite a battle when you begin this process. It really does not like change. And furthermore, it hates to be wrong! Your ego's need to be right will keep you stuck in many behaviors that won't necessarily serve you. The ego's need to be special and unique will keep you separated, isolated, and possibly even quite lonely. Your ego will fight a very intense battle against being subordinated to spiritual values.

If you go so far as to submit yourself to a higher power and dedicate yourself to living a spiritual life, the ego will wage an all-out war. The ego considers itself your source. It neither wants to give up control of your life nor its position of authority over you, nor even recognize that a greater power than it exists in the universe. This is not meant to make you think your ego is an enemy to be battled. But with knowledge comes power, and understanding what you'll be confronted with when you make these changes will allow you to interpret this opposition as actually making progress. Calling upon Spirit through prayer or meditation will connect you with the power to help you overcome anything. Those things we set out to do that are driven by our ego will utilize the ego's natural tendency to use *force* to accomplish its objectives. But when we draw upon Spirit, we draw upon actual *power.* The power of Spirit will always win out over the force of ego. Decide what you want and act as if you already have it. This is having faith.

> *By passionately believing in that which does not exist,*
> *You create it. That which is non-existent has not been*
> *Sufficiently desired.*

-Rumi

CHAPTER 14

Excuses are like Armpits

Excuses are like armpits - everyone has them and they frequently stink (despite our best efforts to deodorize them)! They may sound something like, "Well, I'd be going back to school if it wasn't for my age." Or one that women frequently use, "I'd like to change careers, but my family needs me." Your own excuses are really just descriptions of your circumstances. But your circumstances have nothing to do with your potential. Your potential is infinite.

As a spiritual being you're drawing from a higher power to create the life you want so that you can turn your dreams into reality. It's a rare person who recognizes their own excuses for what they are. Instead we see them as an explanation. It's a description of why we're not doing what we want to do, or we're not where we want to be.

It's easy to recognize this behavior in other people, but much more difficult to see it when we're doing it ourselves. We can easily see it when someone else begins delivering up reasons why they haven't done what they said they wanted to do. There's not a person on this planet that hasn't had to overcome circumstances to get what they wanted. It's called *overcoming* and we all love stories of overcomers. A popular biography of such a person is Oprah Winfrey. We love Oprah because of what she has been able to accomplish despite the harsh circumstances of her early childhood and the odds against which she had to struggle. She gives all of us hope … if she can do it then maybe we can, too.

How did she do it? How did she go from an underprivileged life of an African American young girl in Alabama to one of the wealthiest and most influential human beings in the world? She started by making a decision and confronting her circumstances. There's a tendency to look at successful people and to think that they arrived there by some good fortune that fell upon them.

We weren't there to witness their struggle. It almost seems they might be part of "the chosen few." Which then leads us to worry or conclude that we might not be one of those chosen few. Like not getting the special blessing.

I'm a little embarrassed to admit that there was a time in my life when I considered that maybe there was a curse on me. Things that I was trying to accomplish just didn't seem to pan out. I did everything I thought I was supposed to do yet it didn't produce the hoped-for results. I'd go the extra mile and that wouldn't produce the results either.

Then I realized on a deep feeling level what I had understood on an intellectual level. I had to adjust my intentions. I had not *expected* to get the results I was for which I was working so hard. The realization that I had not been expecting the results led me to realize that I had not been emotionally connected to my intention. I thought that I had an intention, but I didn't feel the desire of it. And since our individual intentions are connected to the larger field of intent - the zero point field from which everything emanates – I was unable to create without making that connection. Actually, I *was* creating something … I was creating more of the same of what I didn't want, because I did have an emotional connection to *not* wanting that. But the universe doesn't hear "not."

A wonderful book on this subject, which I highly recommend, is Dr. Wayne Dyer's *The Power of Intention*. He writes: "Activating the power of intention is the process of connecting with your natural self and letting go with total ego identification." He goes on to say that this process goes on in four stages: the first is discipline, the second is wisdom, the third is love, and, finally, the fourth is surrender. It is in the fourth stage of surrender where intention takes place. The surrender is to something greater than your self - to Spirit. But surrender can be difficult especially when we're busy resisting what we don't want in our life. Resistance will cancel-out surrender at the energetic level.

It's important that we first learn to discipline ourselves (Stage 1). This discipline extends to every area in your life, particularly in some areas in which you feel resistance to it. Discipline has a lot of negative connotations, especially regarding parenting, where it conjures up images of harshness and punitive behavior. But in fact, discipline means "training." It's through training ourselves that we're able to bring our body and our thoughts into alignment with our higher self and with our greater purpose.

Wisdom (Stage 2) entails the knowledge that comes from experience coupled with good judgment and patience. We gain experience by living, doing and making choices. Wisdom comes when we slow ourselves down so that we can make the connection with Spirit and quietly listen.

The third stage in Dr. Dyer's process of connecting with the natural self, that of love, involves our emotional connection with what we're doing; our emotional involvement with the world and our emotional relationship with ourselves and others. Love itself is an emotion that vibrates at a very high frequency. Love has a transformative power. Our own lives can be transformed by the presence of love in our soul, especially as we act from that love. It is communicated to others and out into the Universe and then it returns to us in the same form. We never "love in vain." Love is never lost nor wasted.

If you love what you do, then you're going to be that much better at it. Whether it's housework, paying bills, playing with the kids, caring for the elderly, or weeding your garden - be like the Zen monk who is fully mindful as he scrubs the floor. If you extend love to the people you work with or to your customers, as the beneficiaries of that they'll want to return the kindness. It will come back to you. Often it'll come in the form of money!

Unconditional love is a vibration of such a high frequency that it naturally engages the soul with Spirit. At the point that this communion takes place, your ego is secondary to Spirit once It is running your life. You have arrived at full surrender to Spirit, the force that holds all the potential and which always works for good - the good of all. You don't have to sacrifice in order for someone else to have something. This is not a universe of scarcity but one of abundance. It is not necessary for you to be sick in order for someone else to enjoy health, nor to give everything up so that another won't be poor. These teachings often stem from archaic misunderstandings of the world and nature. You don't have to be poverty-stricken for another to have their needs met. It's not necessary for anyone to forego the blessings and abundance that is available to us all. In fact, since we're all connected, it raises everyone up when anyone prospers. It's the message in the story of "The Loaves and the Fishes" in the Gospel of Matthew. There is always enough no matter what your reality looks like!

The concept of scarcity is actually a lie that we've all bought into and believed. Have you ever worried there is not enough air for you to breathe today? When you see a dog panting, do you worry that he'll use up all of the air? Who worries about whether or not the grass will grow, or the sun will rise or set? We learn to surrender and have faith in the power that runs the universe, even when we're sleeping. Our conscious connection to that power will grow if we make that our intention. Giving our attention to that connection will send more of our energy there. And this will then be reflected in what we have, how we act, and who we become.

There's something that you want for yourself. I invite you to think about it now. Close your eyes and imagine that the thing you want is currently present in your life. I want you to see what your life looks like and how it feels, and what's different now that you have this thing that you wanted. Now notice what the feeling is that you have. There may be one or more feelings. Notice the dominant ones. Notice them all.

Now imagine that this thing that you want is gone from your life. Notice what the feeling is now! Compare the feelings from the two exercises. Which is stronger? If you experienced relief in either of those examples, that's your feedback as to the direction in which you should be heading. If having the thing you want provides relief, then you know that you are on the right track, even if don't know how you're going to achieve it. If imagining being without the thing that you've wanted provides relief, that feedback points to a mistaken goal. If your feelings are positive about what you say you want, you're headed in the right direction. It's that simple.

Ask yourself next, "What will I do if I DON'T be/do/have this?" If you can connect with the feeling of desire for what you want, then you are connecting with the energy stream that will support you and carry you through to its completion. This may be the point where you discover what your excuses have been. Don't allow the tapes that start running in your head to discourage you from having the thing that is in your heart.

If left up to the subconscious mind, you would never experience any outstanding accomplishments in your life. You would be safely ensconced in the routines and habits learned early in life, doing the familiar and comfortable all the way through to the end. Your ability to accomplish anything extraordinary would be completely circumvented by the need for safety and security. And let's not forget the ego's need to be right. Being wrong or looking foolish is like death to the ego, but real death is living a life unfulfilled. Dr. Wayne Dyer says, "Don't die with your song unsung." Every one of us has a song in our heart and we're all here to sing it. People always ask, "What's my purpose?" Be You.

You have a talent and a skill that I don't have. Each one of us has been blessed with our own unique gifts and talents. That is what makes the world so rich. We all bring something different to life. It's conditioning from childhood and adolescence to think that we must all be alike. In the sixties we were all bent on being non-conformists. You can see the irony there - a whole lot of non-conformists conforming to non-conformity. What if nobody thinks like you? What if nobody believes what you believe? Does that make you wrong? Do you have to make up excuses to explain why you're different? Can you just be different?

Allow yourself to be different, and explain yourself to no one. I'm going on the assumption that you will not be harming anyone in the pursuit of your own happiness. The fact is that the happier we are, the more understanding and tolerant we become of others and their differences from us. The more content we are with the path that *we're on*, the less need we have to get others to think the way we do or even to agree with us.

Stop and think of someone who has accomplished great things, whose life you respect. Imagine them trying to make an excuse about why they were late for an appointment. Can you imagine them making up a story and going into details about why they couldn't do what they said they were going to do? It's incongruous, isn't it? Instinctively you know that their ability to create a life of their own satisfaction is one that pulsates with creative energy. There's nothing about that energy that gets caught up in minor concerns, petty objections and excuses. This does not make them special. This just makes them connected. And this is a connection that you can experience. *Where your attention goes, your energy flows.* Telling the truth and being in the creative mode are extremely powerful streams of energy, and as they flow through your life, you're going to be activated and inspired. These streams of energy will draw other ideas to you like a magnet. Stay in that rhythm and flow. Don't get sidetracked by petty concerns. These actions require faith, but the reward is so profound and so quick that this behavior becomes self-perpetuating. Look for your connection to Spirit. The power in that connection creates personal confidence.

Start now. No excuses.

CHAPTER 15

And Your Point Is?

Have you ever known anyone who can't give you a straight answer to a direct question? You can imagine that I see a lot of this as a therapist. Oftentimes people feel as if they have to give the whole long story of what happened and how and why.

People will get off on tangents or some other story as a sidebar, which is relevant in their mind, while the listener is waiting for them to get to the point. This is a pretty common communication problem with people. It's also a reason why so many couples have difficulties talking to each other and don't seem to be able to get any resolution when they disagree. This is a learned behavior and it becomes an ingrained habit.

In a therapy session, I will restate the question, and then together we'll look for the discrepancy between the two conversations. And we also look for the meaning behind the digression. Is it just a habit to answer a question indirectly? Was it not physically or emotionally safe to speak their truth at some time in their past? Or is there an avoidance of issues? Sometimes it might be an unwillingness to be accountable or responsible for one's life. Oftentimes the individual launches into a very long and well-rehearsed, canned version of their life, which has been substituted for their real life. The story has become their identity. You get the feeling that it's not a live discussion. It's a recitation of their story, one that they've told many times before.

One of the most dramatic examples of this is when a patient comes to me with a history of childhood trauma. What I see when they begin to retell their story is a sort of emotional absence. They might even be telling some horrific details of abuse while at the same time smiling. We call that "incongruence." The feelings being demonstrated don't "match up" with the story being told. It is not congruent behavior to smile while recalling traumatic events. It's not hard to see why they have become disconnected from the events. It's too painful to recall the issues. And it is too painful to revisit the feelings. It reveals that they have compartmentalized the information and it's stored out of sight from the rest of their daily consciousness, and particularly away from their feeling self.

Setting aside these examples, there are many people that operate in this way. There is an internal disconnect from how they really feel and when queried they respond with a story. There are files of stories ready to be pulled from rather than operating in the present moment. These individuals pull from their past. We all do it to some extent, but some people primarily communicate in this manner. You know when you encounter one of these people because you feel like you're being talked at, rather than talked to. You might even find your own mind wandering as you listen to their response. And sadly, because they are not really mentally present with you they tend not to notice if your response is delayed or canned. Being mentally present is critical to being fully alive. Staying in the moment is probably the hardest thing that any human being can do.

It's been said that human attention can only remain focused in the present for up to 20 seconds at a time. Then we're off and running! We're wandering around in the past or bolting ahead into the future. Considering this, it's a wonder that we're ever able to create any new memories since it appears we're rarely living in the present!

Therapists rely on their clients to report their internal state. This is generally accomplished through the reporting of events. We know that people who tend toward depressed moods spend more time thinking about the past and their stories will reflect this. On the other hand, people who are anxious are worrying and talking about the future.

It's safe to say that suffering from an anxiety or depressive disorder will compromise the quality your life and your ability to feel alive. In order to live a satisfying, happy life we must be mentally present and our life must feel relevant. Let me define relevance. Relevance is having some sensible or logical connection with something else – having some bearing on issues.

What do I mean by living a life of relevance? While totally subjective, it's the fundamental feeling that *you* matter and that your *life* matters. There is nothing more tragic than someone feeling that his or her life doesn't matter. That's hopelessness. We all must feel that we're here for a purpose - that our very being here makes a contribution.

In the movie, *Shall We Dance?* Susan Sarandon's character tells the private investigator that she's hired to watch her husband, what she believes is the reason people get married: "...because we need a witness. In this world we need at least one person there who can witness our growth and existence. By witnessing us, we're then validated." But what if you don't have a witness (a partner)? Or what if your partner can't give that to you? Then what do you do?

I believe that you must be able to do this for yourself. The meaning of your life must come *from you*. You must decide what that means. You decide what you want in this life. You decide who you want to be. What you want to look like. What qualities you'll possess. How you can make your unique contribution.

Abraham Maslow said, "Self-actualizing people must be what they can be." Since you're still reading this book, that makes you a self-actualizing person. Maslow was saying that it is innate in your being to be the best and the most that you have the potential to be. There is a drive within you to press on and move forward - to experience your full potential. Every human being is capable of this, but not all of humanity operates at the same level of consciousness. According to Dr. David Hawkins' studies in calibrating the levels of human consciousness, 78% of the world's population operates at a lower level of consciousness. He goes on to say that only those people being drawn to a higher level of consciousness are even interested in self-realization.

The Buddha said: "Rare it is to be born a human being. Rarer still to hear the truth. And even rarer still is having heard the truth and then to pursue it." You recognize if you're a pursuer of truth, and that makes it all the more critical that your life feel relevant to you. Begin with elevating your thoughts. There is another saying: "Small minds talk about other people. Average minds talk about events. Great minds talk about ideas." Resolve to be a great mind. One of my mentors once said: *Learn like you'll live forever; live like there's no tomorrow.* Read and study and discuss ideas with like-minded people. Pull yourself up to the next level. Make it your goal to find your relevance or to create your relevance. There are no accidents in the universe. You are not an accident. You are here for a purpose. Find that purpose and live it.

CHAPTER 16

Bringing out the Dirty Laundry

In the last chapter we talked about relevance, and the irrelevance of the rambling storyteller. Very often these stories include drama and this drama gets recycled from one telling of the story to the next. The individual is actually deriving their identity and significance from the painful details. They believe they are a victim in life and they've found some meaning in that. Meaning must be found somewhere within our lives, otherwise we face despondency and hopelessness.

It is much like the identification of the victim with her perpetrators, as in the Patty Hearst story where she was abducted and kept hostage for many weeks and forced to commit a bank robbery. As the granddaughter of publishing magnate, William Randolph Hearst and great-granddaughter of self-made millionaire George Hearst, her on-going ordeal received much attention from the media. Following her kidnapping by the Symbionese Liberation Army (SLA) in 1974, she gained notoriety when she ultimately joined her captors in furthering their cause and was later apprehended after having taken part in the robbery with other SLA members. Clearly, money was not a problem for Ms. Hearst who served nearly two years in prison, before her sentence was commuted by President Jimmy Carter and later pardoned by President Bill Clinton. By the time of the crime however, she had actually begun to identify with her captors. The psychological diagnosis for Ms. Hearst's condition is known as Stockholm Syndrome.

In layman's term, what Stockholm Syndrome describes is a personality so overwhelmed by circumstance or the strength of a dominant personality that it takes on the characteristics and the attributes of the situation or the dominant personality and begins to create a new identity from it. In the case of an extremely weak ego development and low ego strength, the weaker personality will assume the characteristics or even the values of a more dominant personality, as was also demonstrated in the case of the Manson cult.

Charles Manson is the recently deceased American criminal who led the "Manson Family," a quasi-commune of his followers that arose in the late 1960s in California. Though clearly insane, Manson possessed a type of charisma that he used to get his "family" to commit murders. One of the victims, Sharon Tate, was a famous actress who was pregnant at the time of the crime. Manson did not do the actual killings himself, but he was found guilty of conspiracy to commit the Tate-La Bianca murders, which members of the group carried out at his instruction. Through the joint-responsibility rule of conspiracy, he was also convicted of the murders.

Manson is associated with the idea of "helter skelter," the term he took from the Beatles' song by that name and construed as an apocalyptic race war that the murders were intended to precipitate. The term was then used as the title of the book that the prosecutor, Vincent Bugliosi, wrote about the case. Manson's name is now synonymous with insanity.

It is hard to understand how seemingly "normal people" can allow themselves to be seduced into such psychotic madness. According to Dr. Hawkins' scale of consciousness, the madness would score far, far below any emotions or levels of consciousness normally associated with average people. Through the use of drugs coupled with the force of Manson's personality, he encountered no resistance. His seductive appeal no doubt lay in the certainty of his convictions, regardless of their psychotic nature. There is a saying: "If you don't stand for something, you will fall for anything." It is imperative that we define our own moral code and not deviate from it. Dr. Hawkins describes humanity's inherent inability to discern truth from falsehood and this ignorance as the cause of all of mankind's grief. Manson's followers were disconnected from their own values and convictions; Manson, however, was not. We see the tragic results.

Manson's life as a child was a tragic story of extreme neglect and abuse, and ultimately abandonment to the court at age 12 by his young, reputedly alcoholic mother. Bounced back and forth between relatives, he had continued to hope for reunification with his mother and had anticipated it that day in court. Instead, his disappointment at her failure to show up confirmed his experience of rejection, hopelessness and despair, which took over his psyche. The rage that he felt over the depth of his pain was expressed through the psychotic behavior of his psychopathic personality. Ultimately, his depression and overwhelming grief and rage turned to vengeful madness.

Leaving behind the discussion of psychopathology, let's look at normal psychology. Let's explore what's happening when we're focusing on the story of our life, and particularly when we are repeating those stories? As I've intentionally repeated, *where your attention goes, your energy flows*. By continually focusing on the same story it generates more of the same kind of energy in your life through the law of attraction and causes similar situations to recur, repeat, and to recycle themselves. When this happens repeatedly the individual experiencing the repetition feels cursed because they cannot succeed, since the same events and circumstances continue to recycle through their life. What they don't understand is that the cause of it all is their focusing of attention and "thought energy" on those unhappy thoughts. *By re-visiting these negative thoughts and emotions*, those feelings are *revived* and the same frequency of vibration that was operational at the time of the previous (undesirable) experience is *reactivated*. Now the lower vibration causes the actions that flow out of that lowered frequency to produce the same behaviors which *leads to more of the same results*.

This is a difficult point for most people to accept because it suggests that an individual who has suffered unhappy circumstances in their life, particularly a series of them, is being told that it's their fault. Feeling bad already and then blamed for their misfortunes, they protest, "Why would I do that?" The answer is that it's not intentional. You do it by default. By not paying attention to what you're thinking, saying, and feeling, you automatically recycle what comes to mind. And habitually what comes to mind are the memories that threatened your sense of safety in the world. Whenever they're triggered by some apparently threatening event, the nervous system defaults into survival mode and the stories of related painful past events capture your attention. There is some juice, so to speak, that we get from revisiting these dramas. In fact, we are *the star* in the drama and because we sit here to tell the tale, we are the hero. There is triumph in having survived. That is the peak experience. That is the high point, and so to continually retell the story is to get to relive that. But it also means to remain stuck there.

One might argue that history must be studied in order to avoid repeating it. There is a big difference between becoming aware of its existence, and the continual recalling and recycling of the same toxic material.

There are natural laws in the Universe such as the Law of Attraction, to which I have been referring. Another such law is the Law of Perpetual Transmutation, which says that energy moves into physical form and that the images (think "thought energy") you hold in your mind materialize into results in your life. It does make a difference what you *talk* about because first you have to *think* about it.

Another law is The Law of Rhythm that says "the tide comes in and the tide goes out," and that "night follows day" and that good follows bad in a cyclical cycle. If this is true in nature, then why would it be any different for humans who are a part of this natural world? When you're on a down swing, just remember that there are good times coming. Think of them. It will help to balance your emotions by redirecting your thoughts. It can be very empowering.

There is a tendency to constantly compare and contrast. We generally have an idealized version of how things "should have been" and we tend to bemoan our circumstances when they turn out some other way. We find ourselves comparing our current results to our ideal of how it should have been.

Our idea of how it should have been was never a goal. It is simply an arbitrary standard by which we measure our current results. We bring it out at the 11th hour in time to compare it against our current results and then we harshly judge our performance. We tell ourselves, "Nothing ever works for me;" "Other people have all the luck;" or "It always turns out the same."

Rather than comparing your results to an arbitrary ideal, what if you looked at it in the light of how bad it could have been? That sounds a little negative at first glance, but sometimes we need a point of contrast to compare. Recognizing what is positive is a powerful way to connect with that energy stream that delivered it in the first place. Being grateful for what you *don't* have to deal with puts you in mind of the good that you *do* have. Gratitude is a major factor in having a successful life and a satisfying one, too. Gratitude keeps the blessings flowing.

Another law, the Law of Relativity states that nothing is good or bad or big or small until you relate it to something else. Practice relating your situation to something much worse and yours will always look good. Follow that with appreciation and gratitude for what you have. Feel the gratitude. Begin to count your blessings. Look at all the areas of your life *that are* working. Write them out and post them where you can see them every day. Start your day by saying thanks for just waking up, for being healthy, and for having a home and enough to eat, and for all of the opportunities which lie ahead. At this point, you can begin projecting into the future all the possible blessings that are to come.

If you're lonely and wanting friendships, give thanks for all of the people that you <u>are</u> (*will be*, but stated in present tense) magnetically attracting into your life and currently enjoying. If you are worried about money, then give thanks and gratitude for having all of your needs met now. Allow yourself to experience the feelings about the statements you are making - even though they're projections into the future.

Remember your subconscious doesn't know the difference between real or imagined, fantasy or fiction. Experience the feelings as you say the words and they will become a part of your reality. Write down now how you are feeling about life in general. Do this for 30 days and then look at where you started. See the difference. Come back to it after a month and see where you are. You will be amazed at how fast you can reprogram your subconscious mind and change the quality of your life. You can create new habits by continually redirecting your energy toward that which is desired.

Persistence is the key. Continue in this way until you have your new reality.

CHAPTER 17

The Directions for Getting Out of the Box

man·tra (Sanskrit)

1. *Hinduism* -A sacred verbal formula repeated in prayer, meditation, or incantation, such as an invocation of a god, a magic spell, or a syllable or portion of scripture containing mystical potentialities.
2. A commonly repeated word or phrase:

American Heritage Dictionary

At the end of Chapter Six I mention that an attitude has become my mantra- "the time is *now* - get ready for the next thing." A mantra is a phrase we repeat to ourselves to reinforce what we want from life on many levels. There are spiritual mantras, emotional mantras and so on. What has been *your* mantra? You can get an idea of this by looking at who you currently know yourself to be. This will tell you what you've been telling yourself up until now, and as you already know, thoughts become things.

Are you living the life you want to live? This does not necessarily mean in terms of material wealth or luxuries, although let's not exclude that. But in terms of *who you are* – does the world see the "you" that you'd like them to see? Do you yourself know who that person is?

These are such basic questions that it's easy to overlook them or to assume that we have the answers. Most people give more thought to creating a business plan or even a scrapbook project than they do to the development of their self-image, despite the obvious fact that we are the actual vehicle that can take us to our dreams.

A good place to start is by recognizing how special and unique you are if you are even reading this book. The level of awareness necessary to propel someone to even pick up a book on personal development places you in the small group of people who are *self-motivated*. If you take it a step further by implementing new programs or ideas that you have learned from your reading, then quite likely you're in the even more unique group who are *motivators*. The other two groups are the *motivate-able* and the basically *un-motivate-able*. The motivate-able individual can become motivated when in the presence of someone inspiring them, however motivation is lost once that inspiration is out of range. The un-motivate-able description speaks for itself.

Sometimes it helps to just know that we have a slight edge over who we thought we were – it gives us a sort of jump-start of encouragement. Remember, in the end your success will be judged by you and you alone. A life well-lived is ultimately a personal conclusion. Erik Ericson, a psychologist and the author of *The Stages of Life*, theorized that the final stage is when we review our life and decide if it was well-lived, resulting in either integrity or despair. We don't have to wait until the end of our life to figure out if it was well-lived. An assessment right now can reveal your emotional response that can then be used to change your course according to your new ideals.

If you recall from an earlier discussion, we looked at the idea that our thoughts lead to feelings, which then translate into actions, leading to our results. This means that your emotional response to your self-assessment will provide valuable clues as to what you have been thinking about yourself and your image. It's typical of human nature to conclude that what we have just *felt* provides us with important information about our *potential*. This tendency is unproductive because we are actually looping or operating in a circular manner. We can think about our feelings but to spend any extended time there is wasted since it doesn't provide us with any new or constructive information *other than - are we feeling good or bad?* This will clue us in as to whether our thoughts have been constructive or destructive. We always want to go for the better-feeling thought.

When we try something new, it's almost always painful to feel inept or awkward, so we conclude that we aren't good enough and then we withdraw. The problem with this behavior is that we then regard the withdrawal as a failure, and we make a mental note that we failed. According to Maxwell

Maltz in *Psycho-Cybernetics,* this feeds our *automatic mechanism* which is basically goal-striving, and in this case, towards failure. The more that we repeat this behavior, the more we strengthen this failure mechanism.

This is such a waste - our potential is *infinite!* Any results that we're not satisfied with merely provide us with opportunities to fine tune our efforts as we move along the path to achieving our desires. If we will only hang on to that concept of infinite potential, we will then develop dreams worthy of us. The dreams would not only be worth the effort expended, but they would inspire us to persevere to their attainment.

It's critical to make sure that your dreams are big enough. When we downsize our dreams to avoid disappointment, we drain them of the energy needed to manifest. A dream is a thought and thoughts originated the universe. "In the beginning was the word..." (John 1) If, like the Bible says, we really are made in His image, then that means we must have the capacity to create with *our* thoughts. We need to be sure that our interpretation of God does not lead us to see Him as made in *our* image, especially if we believe that we are limited and flawed.

We are spiritual beings first, mental beings next, and then physical beings last. Paramahansa Yogananda called our souls "individualized rays of Spirit." If we could wrap our minds around that then we would stop putting ourselves into tiny little boxes.

I love the Nike ad that asks, "What would you do if you knew you couldn't fail?" That's what we need to be asking ourselves everyday. How would knowing that you could do anything that you set your heart and mind to impact your life? If you really believed it, your life would change. Taking the lid off the box allows the light to flood in, dispelling the shadows where your fears have been hiding and keeping you hostage.

If you knew you'd succeed wildly at anything you did, where would you start? Notice I said, "start" because this is a lifelong process and once you begin, you will never want to stop. Imagine something that you'd like to do more than anything else. Put it to the test: (1) Close your eyes and imagine yourself living this reality – how do you feel? There will be at least two or three feelings, probably some conflicting with each other; ambivalence is normal. (2) Now imagine that this never came to pass and that things are completely unchanged – what feelings do you have now? The contrast between these two states will reveal to you where your desires are. This reveals your purpose!

Everyone needs a purpose, vision and goals. They provide a roadmap for living. It begins with a purpose, the "why" of your life (at least for right now). Without a "why" you don't have a reason for doing the things that fall outside your comfort zone, and you'll stay stuck where you've been. Personal growth occurs *outside* the comfort zone. It's uncomfortable because you're coming up against the old paradigms that keep you right where you are. The paradigms of your ego are constructs designed to maintain the status quo. Sameness equals safety. "No news is good news." Trying new or different behaviors produces discomfort, but this is evidence that you're making progress. As you progress, your clarity on your purpose will increase until it seems as if you've always known that this is what you'd do. And you think, "This wasn't rocket science, why didn't I think of this before?" But it might as well have been rocket science, until the idea came to you. Then it's ...*an idea whose time has come!* Victor Hugo said: "Greater than the tread of mighty armies is an idea whose time has come."

The development of your personal purpose leads to pictures of what your purpose will look like in the outer world. How will your purpose impact your life, your family, your community and the world? Maybe you can't imagine yourself impacting a large sphere of influence, but that's only because we tend to look at our lives up close and personal. Our daily concerns and responsibilities seem to absorb every minute of our waking day, or at least the better part of it. It's hard to imagine how we contribute to the universe in every moment of our existence - but we do. On the most fundamental level, the life-giving air we breathe in contains sub-atomic elements that were exhaled by many other human beings and animals, just as our exhalations will become another being's life-giving air. Biologically and chemically speaking, there are little bits of us in those exhalations which become a part of another person's physical being. The universe is made up of all the same elements, whether found in the earth or in the human body. A study of the carbon cycle provides the understanding that we are intimately linked to the earth and our environment. Carbon constitutes the second largest percentage of the human organism (18%), after oxygen (65%), and is the fourth most abundant element in the universe and considered to be the building block of life (NASA). Like the earth, which is covered over 75% of its surface by water, the human body is also predominantly made up of water (62% by weight – think it's important to drink plenty of good, clean filtered water?); the earth's crust contains 100 or so chemical elements, 8 of which make up 98% of them and 5 of those are also found in the human body, such as calcium, potassium, sodium, magnesium, and iron. Our very existence as part of the human race and as individuals impacts the universe on the most fundamental level.

In Frank Capra's *It's a Wonderful Life*, Jimmy Stewart plays a man whose dreams were deferred to duty so many times that he can't weather the storm of adversity when it hits. Clarence, his guardian angel, arrives just in time to avert his suicide and shows him what his town and family would have looked like without his presence there to touch each one of them. This wonderful film is a feel-good story with an important message; every one of us is important for the part that we play in this life. If we believed this, we would not only be purposeful, productive individuals, but we would also be inspired to create something more, always seeking to expand our experiences.

This seeking to expand leads to our visions. Since we think in pictures, the vision of enacting our purpose in the world is an inspired creative process where we see ourselves *doing our purpose*. When I embraced my own purpose, it generated a stream of visions that elaborated my purpose. I could see in my mind's eye how I could proceed in a variety of directions, all focused on the development of my purpose. The wealth of ideas that come will clue you in to the fact that you're resonating with your purpose, as they abundantly flow into your mind without any real effort on your part.

You can exchange the word "ideas" for "riches" in the following quote by Napoleon Hill, from *Think and Grow Rich,* because riches are just a mental concept or idea: "Riches, when they come in huge quantities, are never the result of hard work! Riches come, if they come at all, in response to definite demands, based upon the application of definite principals, and not by chance or luck."

Your goal is the organization of these visions into a coherent idea and expressed as a definite statement. The creation of the goal statement gives clarity and order to the vision so that action can be taken to produce the desired result. Order and movement are the first two laws of the universe — without these laws, there is chaos and no progress. Your goal is created out of the mental and emotional energy of your purpose and vision. It represents a reaching and stretching towards something more. In fact, if your goal doesn't both excite and make you nervous at the same time, then it's not big enough. It doesn't really matter what your goal is if it's in harmony with your purpose and your values. It will change anyway as it evolves over time, and when it is reached it will be replaced by a new and bigger goal.

The attainment of your goal is not the true value of the process. The real life-changing value of the possession of a goal is its inherent ability to make us grow as we persevere towards its achievement. The power of goal seeking lies in its exercise of our faith as we encounter the obstacles along the way. It's important to realize that there *will* be obstacles. It's the nature of life – it's not a straight line but an organic living coursing that *will* take you to your destination *if you persevere*. Faith is required to complete the journey. You are seeing and believing in something that is in the process of formation. The journey is where the learning takes place and that is when we experience growth. It's not the arrival at our destination but the journey itself that should be appreciated.

One issue that stops many people is the not knowing "how" to accomplish what they want. Here again is where faith comes into play, recognizing that we are spiritual beings equipped with intuition for receiving inspiration from Divine Intelligence. Furthermore, if you can figure out how you're going to attain your goal, then it wasn't big enough to begin with and is actually more an action plan than a goal. It needs to be big enough that when you accomplish it you will know that it was not by chance, but because you had set the goal and made the decision to not quit until you achieved it.

You can't get it wrong – not if you do *something*. Anything we do leads to information that we can gather and evaluate and use to adjust our future course. There is no substitute for the confidence that will grow out of this process. Graduation from "the school of hard knocks" qualifies us as experts in our field.

Your confidence as you make your way towards your goal will grow until you finally see that you have broken out of the box in which you had been trapped. Enjoying your feeling of success and your realization of your capabilities and potential will soon lead you to begin envisioning the next goal. Moving on from here will cause you to confront the next level of paradigms and will move you out of the new box. The directions for getting out of the box are always on the outside of the box!

If a person will advance confidently in the direction of
their dreams and endeavor to live the life they have imagined,
they will meet with success unexpected in common hours.
- Henry David Thoreau

CHAPTER 18

If You Are Not Living on the Edge Then You Are Taking Up Too Much Space

Dr. Lee Poulos, a clinical psychologist and leading authority on the mind says that there are three things that must be present for change to take place. These are desire, expectation, and imagination. Let's talk about desire first. Napoleon Hill said, "...desire is the starting point of all achievement and the first step to riches." In fact, he makes it Chapter One in his classic book, *Think and Grow Rich*. Only Mr. Hill doesn't talk just about desire; he describes having a *burning desire*.

The word desire can be broken into two smaller words: de- sire which is "of" and "to give birth to". There is a creative potential in the concept of desire. A desire is a heightened state of wanting. There are certain things you can look for in your life to discover if your want has become your desire.

The following points will illustrate whether your want has become a desire:
1. The physical results you desire begin to manifest themselves.
2. You see the world through the prism of your desire.
3. You are not affected by outside circumstances.
4. You attract like-minded people.
5. You are awakened and your view of the world changes.
6. Your intuitive factor grows.
7. You easily give up things that are not in harmony with your purpose.
8. Your wants change.
9. You gain emotional control.
10. You move from a competitive to a creative mindset.
11. You have an unquenchable thirst for true knowledge.

At the point where you have an unquenchable thirst for true knowledge, you have actually shifted your desire to a burning desire. That is one of the two telltale signs that you now have a burning desire. You become aware of your oneness with Source, God or Infinite Intelligence. You have also, very likely, changed the way you operate in life in several areas. It all begins with you *wanting* your life to change. You must be willing for your life to change. It has been said that *desire is the unexpressed possibility of an idea wishing to be expressed.*

Each one of us is born with an experience of our specialness. We have within us an experience of something greater than ourselves wishing to be expressed and seeking expression. Yet as we go through life, we lose this feeling. We wrongly assume that all we can ever do is what we've already done. We assume that our history dictates our future and that our current results reflect our potential. We become disenchanted and our negative thoughts draw in more negative experiences.

We must be able to dream. In our dreams are visions of possibilities. As we nurture these possibilities then a desire begins to grow within us. As we nurture that desire it grows and becomes a burning desire. Wanting to be or do something more is the starting point. Then comes expectation. Be sure that your expectations are *aligned* with your desires. As I've shared with you before there was a time in my life when I had great desires but my expectations were not in alignment. I found myself entertaining expectations of failure. People wouldn't come to hear what I had to say. No one would want what I was offering. These were fears of the future based on negative past experiences carried forward into the present. It's a "worst case scenario" situation. I'd entertain the thought of failure as though I would somehow protect myself from experiencing it. Of course, understanding the Law of Attraction we know that what I did was to attract more of the same to myself. There was no curse on my life. I was cursing myself by continually recycling the negative thinking.

The whole idea of having a Plan B falls into this category as well. Plan B reveals that you don't have faith in Plan A. You don't expect plan A to succeed. Don't allow weeds of doubt to grow in your mind. Guard your mind and make sure your thoughts are only of the result you desire. It takes practice to change this habit, but it becomes easy as you practice. You will replace the old "bad habit" of negative thinking and focusing on failure with a good habit of expecting success.

Imagination is the final component. Thomas Edison said, "Imagination is the workshop of the mind." This is where you can literally create mental movies of your success. See yourself attaining your desired goal. Remember your subconscious mind doesn't know the difference between fantasy and fiction. Your subconscious mind can be used to bring about the successful attainment of anything that you desire and can visualize.

There's a true story from a number of years ago about a railroad worker who found himself trapped in a refrigerator boxcar. Once he discovered he was in for the night without apparent hope of rescue, he began to anticipate the effects the cold would have on his body. He knew that he could not survive the night dressed as he was and without a blanket to protect him from the cold. Throughout the night he was journaling on a scrap of paper. He described his physical condition as the night wore on and he got colder and colder. He was unable to write any longer. At the end of the note, he acknowledged that he knew that the end had come. The next morning when they opened the car they found his note alongside his body. Though he *had* frozen to death, the refrigeration unit in that car was malfunctioning and it never got below 55 degrees that night. It was the power of that man's mind that caused him to freeze to death. If it's possible to think oneself into death, wouldn't it be possible to think oneself into a life? And would it really be *that* hard to have a goal and see it come to fruition?

To advance in life we must move forward into the unknown. We must be willing to take risks. If we never leave the realm of the known, then we are not exploring and we're never moving into new territory. We must stretch ourselves, and, yes, it *is* scary! (Scary and exciting are emotions that feel very similar in the body.) Fear can be a great motivator, too, especially when doing nothing can have worse consequences than doing almost anything.

Everything in the universe is in motion. It is constantly expanding. If we want to expand and grow we must vacate the space we're occupying. This creates a vacuum that must then be filled. If everything in the universe is constantly expanding and in motion, then how can we humans as part of that universe be any different? When we're stagnant, not growing, staying the same, it creates an unnatural condition. We just don't feel right. We become restless and frustrated. We look backwards. We regress. We complain. Often, we blame it on our current circumstances. More often we'll blame it on our partner, or maybe the ex.

No matter what your circumstances are, if you're not happy, take responsibility for that. Look at your life. Change it. Just do something different. Take a chance. The worst mistake you can make is to do nothing. Any decision you make will move you to a new space and a new level of awareness. Its okay to be afraid, just don't let your fears stop you. It's been stated that the greatest motivator for many is the fear of loss, rather than the desire for gain. If that feels true for you, then imagine losing the hope or the opportunity to ever have the life you truly desire; let the fear of experiencing *that* loss push you forward and out of your comfort zone.

Take a few steps forward then pause and assess your circumstances - reevaluate your course and move forward again. There is no perfect way to do this life. As long as you stay in motion and keep your expectations focused on your desire, then you are living life. You are doing what you came here to do. You are creating experiences, learning from them, and creating more experiences.

Dr. Martin Luther King, Jr. said, "If you can't fly, then run; if you can't run, then walk; if you can't walk, then crawl; but whatever you do, you have to keep moving forward."

Get in front of your life. It's sort of like scrambling to get in the first car on a rollercoaster. Don't miss any of the twists and turns. Be awake and experience the thrill of the ups and down. It really is, after all, a very short ride.

CHAPTER 19

Rewriting History

In my work with trauma clients, I know that the one thing that most haunts the client who has suffered from earlier traumatic events is the *perception they have about themselves* because of what's happened to them. For those struggling with Post Traumatic Stress Disorder (PTSD), it isn't necessarily the event that is torturing them but their perception about how they handled themselves and what they believe it says about *them*. They're left with a core belief that they are basically defective, unlovable, or invisible, and sometimes live with the constant belief that they're about to die. Trauma victims have almost always shifted the blame over to themselves and have subsequently developed certain behaviors to compensate for the shame that was put into them.

The old saying "time heals all wounds" does not apply in these cases. It *does not spontaneously heal* in a person with PTSD. With trauma, there are neurophysiological responses that occur in the body at the time of the traumatic event that caused their thought processes to freeze or stick in place. These responses continue to loop or recycle throughout their life

In fact, time exacerbates the trauma, adding more stress on top of the original stressor. Traumatic events, particularly those that evoke the fear of one's own death, create such a strong physiological response that oftentimes the actual personality is impacted and even changed. The traumatic memory is frozen in the nervous system, where it is frequently triggered by seemingly ordinary events that set it off again. This could be a smell or sound that reminds their system of the original event. Or it could be an interaction with another that triggers old feelings like rejection or shame, leading to overwhelming emotions that take over the present moment, shooting the person back to that moment of the original event.

The alarm goes off as the nervous system recognizes potential danger and begins looping the original defense responses. These responses might be anything from fight-flight-freeze, hide/avoid, submit/collapse, to dissociate. Whatever the body used to defend itself in the original traumatic event will be what will start running. This is a neurophysiological process that the conscious mind has no control over and only recognizes that it's up and running (again) once it's underway. It takes over the person and although they may be aware that their response is out of proportion to the event at hand, there's nothing they can do but ride it out until they (their nervous system) can return to a feeling of safety. The major blow of the original trauma impacts the body and emotions and carries over from one day to the next, along with whatever current unresolved stressors occur. The individual's ability to sleep is disrupted, compromising their ability to function in daily life and continuing to negatively affect their nervous system. Their resources to deal with daily stressors are not what they would have been without the trauma, both physically and psychologically. It becomes compounded with each passing day.

Rapid eye movement or REM sleep state is disrupted with PTSD. That's the time during sleep when your eyes are moving and you're processing the day's stressors. When the REM sleep state is disturbed, the individual awakes in the morning still *carrying* the stressors of the previous day. There is a cumulative affect with time and it is easy to see why I say that time does not heal this wound.

The nutshell version of how to resolve that trauma involves the patient identifying the negative belief(s) they have about themselves while remembering the unfinished emotions of the original traumatic moments. These emotions are carefully contained within the therapy session, and this remembering happens only when they feel safe and secure enough to step into the memory. Exercises designed to bring them into that state of readiness and to maintain that state allows for stepping-into the memory. By allowing the expression of the frozen emotions and unfinished feelings, there is a discharge of the trapped energy that has looped for so long, and the patient experiences a felt sense of relief and completion. The memory is not forgotten but its emotional charge has dissipated.

Ultimately the person arrives naturally and organically at a *new self assessment* that is forgiving and compassionate and allows for peace when remembering. The prior behaviors that were used to compensate for the negative beliefs are no longer needed and they fall away naturally; the individual will describe catching them self behaving differently, no longer having the same old response.

The DSM - Diagnostic and Statistical Manual of Mental Health

Disorders - states that PTSD is dependent on a few primary causes, one of which is experiencing a threat to one's own life. Another is witnessing firsthand a threat to or the death of another person; this event is an extraordinary one that falls outside the realm of normal human experiences.

In my work, I've seen that people are not all traumatized by the same things. Depending on the age of the individual some situations may not fit that earlier mentioned diagnostic criteria. A young child, for example, may experience a separation from mother as a traumatizing event. Violence that is witnessed by a child can be as traumatizing as experiencing it directly. Neglectful caregiving also creates insecurity in the developing psyche, and this includes parents who are emotionally vacant and un-attuned to the needs of their child. If a child has lived with multiple caregivers, particularly before the age of three, they may be exposed to life-changing trauma.

Every child comes into this world hard-wired for attachment and they're seeking to bond with the mother whose heartbeat they heard while in utero. Every infant needs "good enough mothering" which means that most of the time they'll feel unconditionally loved, supported, and protected. When this doesn't happen, they don't blame the parents – they blame themselves. This is learned through experience and occurs even during the preverbal period. This leads to behaviors to compensate for their own failure to get their parent's love. Of course, these behaviors rarely work but they become automatic nonetheless and will show up in future adult romantic attachments. It's human nature to experience your partner through the filter of your parent-child relationship, but especially so with the unresolved stuff. Couples in high-conflict relationships are often like two little kids, each one trying to get the other to meet their needs.

PTSD is not always clear-cut in its symptoms. It may include a cluster of symptoms that are each a diagnosis in itself, for example, anxiety and/or depression. A patient may be diagnosed with clinical depression or generalized anxiety, which may actually be symptoms of a pre-existing PTSD. This is not always evident to clinicians who do not specialize in trauma. It's only recently that PTSD came into American awareness with returning Vietnam veterans and later with Desert Storm and Iraq veterans, and has lately received even more attention. It's becoming understood that early life experiences have the ability to profoundly impact the way you see your life. It's as if our experiences are a frame around this thing we call life. A frame in the traditional sense is designed to set a picture off or even enhance it. It also creates the boundary so the viewer knows where the picture ends and it can be separated from its surroundings.

Our life experiences are like that, putting a boundary around ourselves and framing our life so that we say that we are "like this." I invite you to expand your thinking here. You can reframe your life at any moment you choose. A "reframe" describes the process of making a conscious decision to change the way you look at a situation and intentionally choosing to interpret it in a more positive way.

How have you framed yourself? If it's been by your past, then has it been limiting you? Is it a positive story or a negative one? If it is negative, what is the point of the negativity? Is it because you've learned lessons? Is it to illustrate where you've come from or what you've overcome? Or has it become a story of victimization? Regardless of what has happened to you, you decide the story. Don't allow anyone to have that power over you. When you react emotionally you know that you've given your power away. It's *your* life and your interpretation of the events. Let your interpretation lead to your own emotional response.

If you were to tell me that I'm stupid and ugly, I might tell you that those are unkind words and I don't appreciate them. But I would know that it doesn't make me stupid or ugly, unless on some deep level I already think that. I may fear that I'm stupid or ugly, in which case your words would resonate with something I already believe. Do you see how the interpretation takes place within *me*? I have to first give it my time and attention before it can even impact me.

I'm not suggesting here that if you have been mistreated or abused that those things didn't really happen to you. That would be ludicrous, and disrespectful. Such events that occur in the life of a child are tragic and heartbreaking. But I ask you what you want to do with that now? Will you let that story define your life and limit you? How much longer are you willing to let the drama recycle? If you spent years trapped and powerless to do anything about it, it's time now to take back your life … and your power.

If you're stuck in harboring anger, resentment and un-forgiveness in your heart against someone - just know that it cannot touch another person. They can't feel it. They have no experience of it. It's like the metaphor of the anger being like a hot coal carried in the palm of someone's hand and only they can feel the burn. It is only the one who is the bearer of the un-forgiveness who truly suffers. To forgive is to forgive *oneself*. Remember the example earlier of the traumatized individuals and their negative self-thoughts and beliefs about their world. The unforgiving person is the one who is stuck with it.

There is nothing to be gained by holding on to feelings of un-forgiveness. It teaches the perpetrator nothing. It is not up to you to bring that person to justice. In fact, the Law of Cause and Effect (also known as karma) says that whatever you send out into the universe comes back. Action and reaction are equal and opposite. If you believe that then you'll realize that you cannot afford to put anything out into the universe that you do not want to come back to you.

As for the perpetrator, the universe will take care of them according to *their* own karma. That might even lead you to have an experience of compassion for them, seeing the damage they have done to their own lives. A wonderful source of inspiration on this topic is *A Course in Miracles*. The primary theme is about the power of forgiveness and love. Unconditional love is the doorway into the life of the mystic. All the world's truly evolved souls have passed through this doorway of unconditional love. Socrates said, "All men choose what they believe is good." Jesus, Buddha and Krishna each taught that "All error is due to ignorance." And during his crucifixion, Jesus prayed, "Forgive them, Lord, for they know not what they do" (Luke 23:34). Once we finally understand that people are operating at their own level of consciousness - that they're doing the best they can with *what they have to work with* - it makes forgiveness and unconditional love almost effortless. People don't set out to ruin their lives or yours, or to be the most awful they can be. Regardless of how society may have judged them, they were doing the best they could with what they knew. This single concept can free you from the trap of being the judge of another's life. And it can lead you to the next level of consciousness where you can experience the compassion that leads to unconditional love.

Albert Einstein was quoted as saying, "The significant problems we have cannot be solved at the same level of thinking with which we created them. "How can we judge what is good using the same mind that created the problematic behavior? It is very difficult if not impossible for us to see our problems for ourselves. That's why it's critically important to have people in your life that will tell you the truth. They should be trusted people you can count on to give you feedback to help you evaluate where you are and help you to make necessary changes. This is what a therapist does, or a life coach or best friend, assuming you've picked people who are willing to be honest with you!

So, if you are ready to make changes, the first step is to reframe the past. If a part of your life was a disappointment or maybe created shame for you, then now is the time to make that reframe. Start by taking a look at your experiences and asking yourself, "What did I learn from it and how has it made me into the person I am today?" For every negative aspect there is a positive side to it. If you think you are shy and untrusting, turn it around and see this quality as "cautious and careful." It may not change how the behavior looks on the outside, but it puts it into a positive frame and this different perspective can make you feel less stuck. You will begin to recognize the strengths that you possess.

People learn best when they are happy and relaxed. Being harsh on yourself does nothing to improve your situation. Relax, lighten up and look for what's positive in every aspect of your personality. If you are an angry person, then reframe it as someone who is assertive and willing to stand up for yourself. If you are accustomed to behaving as a doormat, then reframe it as someone who is "patient, understanding and tolerant." You have nothing to lose by this process and everything to gain. The point is to build up your self-esteem and feelings of self-worth. This will energetically elevate you to become ready to take more assertive and positive action in your life.

As you do this you will begin to connect with the energy that becomes available to you. It's a creative energy and a power. You will feel empowered. This is what is really meant by empowerment - not something that drops down on you from the sky. Empowerment is something that you step into.

After you've done some of this reframing you will begin seeing the areas you wish to change first. Having reframed and renamed some previously negative quality, you'll then be able to consider what you'd like to replace it with. If in the past you may have been angry or overly assertive about your rights, now as you begin to feel more balanced, you'll find that you have the energy to offset that with the more desirable behavior. Create an affirmation that states something like "I am patient and tolerant at all times and in all circumstances." Then you can begin to look for opportunities to put that into play. Repetition is the key to learning. Practice, practice, practice. Continual rehearsal of these behaviors and ways of thinking will cause them to become second nature to you and a part of your new conditioning. They will become your new habits.

It's true that, "It's not what happens to you, but what you do with what happens to you." Lessons were gleaned from the difficult experiences in your life. Behaviors and attitudes developed and have led you onto the path you've been travelling. But at any point along the way you can change that path. If you're not satisfied with where you are or with what you've done, take a look at where you are in this moment, the book you're reading, the new ideas you are entertaining, and ask yourself, "Where can I go from here?"

CHAPTER 20

How Do You Know When You Need a Professional?

Let's assume that you've tried reframing your life and you've come to the conclusion that, as much as you don't like to admit it, you still feel like you were a victim. You've tried to see it in a positive light and to acknowledge the lessons that you've learned, yet you feel unable to let go of the feelings or resentments. You feel stuck. What do you do next? This is probably the time you should seek out a professional.

In my early years as a therapist, I also had a therapist. I now have a personal coach. We need the vantage point of an outside observer. We need to be able to see ourselves, and what we're doing, in another light and from another perspective. The expression, "You can't see the forest for the trees" means that we're just too close to the individual aspects of the forest (the trees) to be able to see the big picture. In the same way, we're too close to our own life to be able to see it objectively. It goes back to what Einstein said, and it bears repeating here: "The significant problems we have cannot be solved at the same level of thinking with which we created them."

I firmly believe if we're focused on our personal development, that with enough time we can all eventually grow into a greater level of self-actualization. The exception to this as I've explained before is a history of trauma; the symptoms of PTSD generally worsen with time. Otherwise, for the rest of us who no longer want to stay small and play it safe, but are feeling drawn to grow and learn, to expand into playing in a bigger way ... we must ask ourselves if we're satisfied with our progress? Based on your history, how long will it take to move to the next level? Do you have that kind of time? Or are you anxious to get started now?

This might bring up all sorts of fears and terrors as you imagine confronting the past or the unknown. That's okay. Actually, the fear tells you that you are onto something. Don't let that fear stop you. Remember, "Courage is bravery in the face of fear." If you had no fear, you'd have no need for courage. It's not about abolishing the fear, but about conquering it by stepping into it. And that's when the power of a personal support person can make all the difference. Remember I told you how human beings are hard-wired for attachment? Having someone there to provide encouragement, support, comfort and companionship along the journey will activate the neurochemicals of oxytocin, prolactin and the mu opioids that create feelings of worthiness, deservingness and the warmth of belonging. That equates to an experience of internal secure attachment within oneself. That's the secure base of operation for extending ourselves in life. That means that we do best when we're not alone.

So let's look at how to go about finding the right qualified professional to help you. We always start with referrals from people we trust. But I feel it's really important to take a look at the source of the referral. Let's say you've gotten a referral from a family member - are they getting the kind of results that you'd like? Are they a good judge of who would be the right fit for you? Do your homework and find out who are the most successful people in your area providing the service that you seek. Uncle Joe's neighbor's cousin who sells real estate part-time might be a really nice guy, but how does Uncle Joe's portfolio look? If you have a very successful friend or relative, by all means, go to them first and get their referrals. But it brings to mind the old sayings, "the proof is in the pudding" and "the fruit is on the tree."

If you don't have anyone in your inner circle or your network, the next places to find help are professional associations. If you are looking for individual supportive therapy, then those professionals most highly trained in providing one-on-one psychotherapy are Licensed Marriage and Family Therapists, Licensed Professional Counselors and Psychologists. Marriage and Family Therapists tend to come from an educational background that deals with families, groups, and relationships. Their training is focused on the impact of the relationships throughout an individual's life, especially including the family of origin. Your relationships today tend to reflect your earliest relationships as you attempt to resolve your earlier issues through the repetition compulsion.

Although this doesn't work, there is a natural compulsion to do this. Working with a professional who understands the patterns and dynamics of relationships can help reveal to you the way out of this compulsive pattern.

To find a Licensed Marriage and Family Therapist (LMFT) in your area you can contact the American Association of Marriage and Family Therapists (AAMFT) by visiting their website www.aamft.org to locate therapists by zip code. In California there is a state specific organization called The California Association of Marriage and Family Therapists or CAMFT. Their website is www.camft.org. Other states have their local associations.

Once you've identified two or three different therapists, then it is recommended to interview them to see if they are a good fit for you. Some therapists will take a few minutes to talk to you on the phone prior to the first meeting; you can see if it feels like a suitable match. The first session is generally about history taking but it is also an opportunity for both client and therapist to see if you are a good fit for a working relationship. It is very important to see if there is what feels like a potential for friendship. Notice that I said *potential* for friendship," not to imply that a friendship will ensue. Ethically and legally the therapist must maintain certain boundaries to maintain a healthy therapeutic relationship. The more comfortable you are with the therapist, the more likely you'll feel safe to open-up and let them see inside you. Revealing the more vulnerable parts of your personality and your experiences, and being willing to share the painful parts is what happens in good therapy. It is through this level of honesty that the therapist can understand and help you work through the issues.

Don't make the assumption that because the person is a professional that they can read your mind or know the unspoken parts of your story. You must provide that information and if you can't or don't because you are not comfortable doing so, then you must continue to look for the professional with whom you can find that level of comfort. This is, after all, your *life*. And if you take this journey with someone qualified, you should never need to cover this ground again. Be selective and pay attention to your gut. Therapists are people and they have personalities just like the rest of the population. Be sure to find one whose personality is a fit with yours. A good therapist will create a safe holding space for you. Look for someone with whom you feel comfortable enough to be able to move right in and address the issues that you need to address.

If you believe you suffer from PTSD, then you will want to find a trauma therapist who can help you do the deep work needed to clear it out. The

Comprehensive Resource Model© (CRM) is the most effective and thorough approach that I know of and which can safely help even the most traumatized. It works with Complex PTSD, as well as DID. It's also great for general issues besides trauma. In any case, CRM is relatively quick in producing relief.

EMDR is another treatment method for trauma. The focus on the traumatic incident makes it especially effective with single incident traumas. After the resolution you may want to continue in therapy for a bit in order to process the changes, or at that time find a personal life coach.

There are other times when we need a professional but not necessarily a mental health professional. When we want to get in control of our finances, buy a house, or find a new doctor or dentist, we need to seek out these professionals for our "team". Robert Kyosaki, famed author of the *Rich Dad Poor Dad* series, believes that we should all have our own team of personal advisors. From legal to tax to investment issues, this group becomes our own personal resource team. Each person on that team should be someone with whom you feel comfortable sharing your personal business and not intimidated; you must trust them. While reading Kyosaki's book, I looked at my own team at that time and saw that my CPA was not someone I could talk to easily or comfortably, so I wasn't getting my questions answered. Worse yet, her responses to my questions often made me feel dumb (yet I was paying for this service ... so maybe I was a little dumb!). So, I found a new CPA and now I always look forward to talking with her ... and I get all my questions answered.

Don't settle for less than satisfying relationships in any area of your life. We're taught as children to obey authority and respect our elders. This tends to carry over into our adult life in our conditioning not to question and to just tolerate those uncomfortable feelings. That no longer serves you and it probably never has. There is no constructive value in continuing in any relationship in which you are not having your needs met. Sometimes in a professional relationship, you need to remind yourself that you are the customer.

Be discriminating and do your homework. You're interviewing people to advise you in your life. One more saying: "Your life is not a dress rehearsal" - this is the actual performance.

CHAPTER 21
You Can't Out-Perform Your Self Image

Your results are dictated by your level of awareness, which is a direct reflection of your self-image. Who you *think* you are is who you will be. Until you think differently, nothing will change.

Level of awareness is not the same as knowledge, but it comes out of our self-knowledge. It's more about feeling, but not entirely. It's like a reflection of our attitude born out of our experiences. Level of awareness is dictated by our subconscious mind where everything is stored; therefore, it's mostly below our level of awareness. What? Our level of awareness is dictated by something that is *below* our level of awareness?

You may want to return to the discussion in Chapter 9 on reprogramming your mind or Chapter 17 for getting out of the box. You may be thinking, "Thanks for sharing, Avis, but I've tried CDs and seminars, etc. and nothing has changed. Is there some trick or technique to facilitate change?" The answer is yes!

Dr. David Hawkins, in his book *Power versus Force* discusses the kinesiology exercise known as muscle testing, as a way to discover the truth on any subject. Through muscle testing, it's possible to discover what your subconscious mind holds to be true. In this way you can uncover what your paradigms are. What are the conditionings or habits that have been formed since early childhood of which you may be unaware, but which dictate your actions and the outcome in your life?

All along I've been telling you that the way to discover what is "the truth" in your subconscious mind is by entertaining a new idea and then identifying any internal resistance. It's when you encounter this conflict that you become aware that you are holding on to a paradigm that is not currently serving you. That is also known as having a "limiting belief."

Imagine if you were able to discover proactively, before encountering another incident of resistance, that you've been holding onto a belief that's been limiting you in reaching your dreams and goals. Rather than guessing at what it is, it's possible to find out specifically what's holding you back. Once you discover what it is, this immediately elevates your level of awareness.

Let me give you an example of how this works. Let's say you suffer from anxiety when it comes to test taking. Every time you're facing a test you begin to suffer from anxiety so much that when the test time arrives, your anxiety is so high you can't focus or you may even freeze. This causes a less-than-desired result - reinforcing your fear that you are not smart enough. It is possible to have an above average IQ and still have this self-limiting belief that you are not intelligent. You'll believe it because of your performance.

So now you've identified this problem area and yet you don't know how to go about changing something that resides so deep within you. This is where muscle testing comes in. Dr. David Hawkins made the connection between *truth* and the *power* that naturally accompanies it. He also connected that which is *not true* (a subtle difference from "false") with the *force* that usually accompanies it. You may have experienced this when you have felt that you've been pushing to make something happen and it wouldn't go and then later you discover the obvious reason it wouldn't flow. Versus those times when you were just "in the flow."

Dr. Hawkins has some wonderful instructive video material available on DVD for the exact procedures for muscle testing. Check out the sources in the back of this book to get further instructions on correctly using this procedure.

The way it works is that it usually takes two individuals. One is the tester and one is the testee. The testee stands with eyes closed and with arms at side and then extends one arm parallel to the ground. The tester places one hand on the shoulder of the testee to steady the person, and their other hand is placed on the extended arm just above the wrist. Using two fingers atop the wrist and the thumb underneath it, this will allow the tester to exert gentle "testing" pressure on the arm. At the exact moment of the muscle test, the testee will be directed to "resist" or "be strong" while the pressure downward on the wrist will quick and firm, but not too intense.

The movement by the tester is short and quick and without exertion of too much strength. It's simply to look for resistance in the arm. When a true statement is made (one that is life-affirming), energy will flow through the arm and there will be a resistance that keeps the arm exactly parallel to the floor and very strong. When a statement is made that is not true (not life-affirming), then the strength is lost or weakened due to lack of energy flow, and the arm is unable to resist the pressure by the tester; it will be easily pushed down toward the floor.

It is necessary to make statements when doing muscle testing, as opposed to asking questions. It doesn't work to pose questions because you are looking for the truth within the issue. Start with a simple statement by the testee, such as "My name is ____," as the tester instructs to "resist" and immediately applies quick pressure on the arm. Because the statement is true, the arm will appear strong as the energy flows and the arm will resist and be immovable.

Next the testee will state a name that is not theirs. Again the tester will say, "resist," but this time because the statement lacks truth, the energy does not flow and there will be a loss of strength; the arm will move toward the floor. This does take some practice, which is why the videos are recommended for viewing, in order to perfect the technique. Playing with statements such as one's own name and an imaginary one is an excellent test for how you are progressing with the technique. A muscle test will reveal the truth of something. It does not reveal *degrees of truth* and it does not *answer questions*. The information is drawn from the zero point field, which is where everything that has ever occurred is stored and can be drawn upon using this technique.

You cannot predict the future, nor can you test with self-serving, non-integrous intentions, so don't bother muscle testing for the winning lottery numbers because it won't work. Anything that can be made into a statement can be tested for its truthfulness. You can test your ability to do the process with a variety of statements such as "I am a boy/girl," "I am 25 years old/my actual age." Experiment with the sorts of statements that are either absolutely true or false to see how you're progressing with the technique.

Once you've established a degree of comfort with the technique, then you can begin to make statements about yourself to discover what's true and what isn't.

Returning to our example about test taking anxiety, you might start with the statement "I am an intelligent individual" and test that. What you're actually determining when making these I statements is whether or not your subconscious mind holds them to be true. If in this example your IQ is 125 and your muscle test proves to be weak to the statement "I am an intelligent individual," then that will reveal that *your subconscious mind* believes that you are not an intelligent person. Now you have identified that belief and you can move to the point where you can rectify it.

One way to do this would be to use the tapping discussed in Chapter 13.

Psych-K© is another that uses the following simple exercise to re-wire the circuitry. This technique involves stimulation of the left and right hemispheres of the brain, which when done alternately or concurrently will stimulate whole-brain functioning. There is a very simple technique that can be done by sitting down and crossing the legs at the ankles; crossing hands at the wrists, palms facing each other and entwining the fingers. Closing the eyes, sit quietly and silently repeat the desired statement (the one which you would prefer for your mind to hold as the truth) repeatedly for one to three minutes. You'll know the process is complete when you find your mind losing interest in the statement and starting to wander. At that time, uncross arms and legs and the tester then conducts the muscle test while the testee says the statement aloud. If the testee is not strong to the statement, then repeating the process one more time will generally bring about the desired result.

By repeating the statement over and over while the legs and arms are crossed (creating a cross lateral stimulation of the brain), the result is a reprogramming in the subconscious mind. It's much like you would save a change in a document by hitting "Save" on your computer. It has "written over" the changes. The next time you open that document you only see what has been overwritten. In the same way your subconscious mind has been overwritten and that becomes the new operating truth. Because it has occurred at the level of the subconscious mind you may not notice the change until you catch yourself operating differently. Sometimes it might even be others who will notice the changes in your behavior.

One client had such a fear of heights she could not take an elevator or escalator. At work whenever she had to meet clients she had to run down the stairs of a multi-story office building to meet them. After working on this issue with this process, she was on vacation with her husband and sister in Las Vegas. They were riding together in a glass elevator in one of the high-rise hotels - they were astonished that she was doing this, but she seemed oblivious that she had done anything different. That's because she was operating according to the new pattern in her subconscious (which directs our bodies) and had no recall of her former fear.

Sometimes it is such a natural change like this that you won't even be aware of the rewrite. Generally, you will be aware of a freedom or release in an area that formerly felt limiting to you. The potential using this technique is unlimited. You can literally create within your subconscious mind the conditioning and the belief system that you would like to predominate to advance you in the direction of your goals. Any area of your life can be addressed in a positive manner. You can create statements around abundance and energy, initiative, creativity, friendship, and love, understanding all the while that it is your subconscious mind you are programming.

The statements must relate to you personally. This technique cannot be used to control others nor for any purpose that would be unethical.

The question may come up for you, "Isn't it un-integrous, or untruthful, to be programming myself with statements that are not held to be true by my mind?" Not as long as what you're trying to reprogram is in your highest and best interest and in the service of growth. Spirit will always support what is abundant, life-giving, expansive, creative, beautiful and loving. These qualities are always in harmony with the Universe and with Spirit.

This is a good example of how we can know something intellectually but not know it on an emotional level, at the level of the heart. When you know something in your heart you can state: "I know that I know that I know."

You may be thinking this is an absurdly simple remedy for a complex and deep-seated problem. I initially felt that way myself. But in order to learn the technique, I needed to apply it first to myself. I can say that I have personally derived tremendous benefits from these techniques.

There are core beliefs that everyone holds which are deeply imbedded in our psyche. They are rooted in our subconscious mind. We're unaware of what these beliefs are but every day they drive us and limit us as well. You can use your imagination as to what qualities might be necessary for you to possess in order to pursue the life you dream of having. Identify what those qualities are and then muscle test to see if you possess those qualities and characteristics. If you don't currently possess them you can apply the technique described, the whole brain approach, in order to download into your psyche the programming you would prefer, in order to realize your full potential.

The technique I've described to you involves muscle testing and finding out what is true within your subconscious mind. There is a part of the mind that is connected with the zero point field and that is Mind - the super conscious. That is the repository of the Truth that exists and that is accessible to everyone. For example, you may be dating someone and may feel torn because on some level you feel that the relationship may not be good for you, yet you feel an attraction. It's possible to determine through muscle testing if this relationship is in your highest good or best interest. Again, employing the muscle testing technique you would formulate a statement that could be tested for true or false that sounds like, "It is in my highest and best interest to be in an intimate relationship with John." At that point you would muscle test. A weak response indicates that it is NOT in your best interest to be in that relationship.

It is important to be clear and specific when muscle testing. You cannot be general or vague in any way. For example, if you wanted to find out if a job opportunity was in your best interest, you would have to be specific and state which conditions would be in your best interest. For example, "This new job opportunity offers me the best opportunity for advancement and promotion," and then you would muscle test that. Then you would go to the work environment. "This new job opportunity offers me a work environment which is in my highest and best interest." And then you would test that and so on. It is best to test a series of short specific statements instead of a cluster of multiple ideas, which might individually test out with different results.

If you practice the techniques I've discussed in this book such as meditation, prayer, contemplation, etc. you will find that your intuition will become more developed. As you muscle-test, you may begin to find that you can sense or intuit the answer before you see the answer via the muscle test. You can see how practical the application of this method is. You may be wondering how to have a greater utilization with this technique, and how to do this alone if you don't have a partner to be the tester.

You can take your index finger on your left hand and touch it to your thumb making an O-ring. Do the same on your right and link them together like a chain. When testing the muscle response, try to pull the two "O" rings apart. You will find that the chain does not break for a strong and positive response, yet they snap apart and the chain is broken for a weak one. This is a way for you to employ these techniques on your own and utilize the knowing of what is in your highest and best interest in every situation. You can also use a pendulum to ask basic questions through establishing which direction the pendulum swings for either "yes" or "no."

You will reinforce the development of your intuition, as your testing confirms it. If you doubt your test, go back to the name test and reestablish that you are testing correctly. State "My name is…" and test and then state a false name…and you can verify that you are indeed on track.

Sometimes when doing this process, you can get very excited because it is very exciting stuff! That can mess up the test. You'll be strong on everything. You'll get the same response no matter what you're asking. Just sit down in the whole brain position and quietly allow your system to re-balance itself. Return to the name test to verify that your energy levels are back to normal.

I was originally skeptical of this balancing technique, and if it weren't for the fact that I personally experienced a feeling of relief from the constraints of some self-limiting beliefs, I would never have utilized it with clients and friends. When introduced to it, however, I already understood the power of stimulating both sides of the brain through the use of EMDR with trauma patients, and fortunately didn't dismiss it as overly simplistic and too good to be true. I personally use this technique on a regular basis, whenever I feel the need arises.

My own experience had such a profound impact on my own life. I discovered that I was holding on to two conflicting beliefs. One was "I love myself" and the other was "I hate myself." It really was as if I was going through life with one foot on the gas and the other foot on the brake. The feeling of relief and freedom that came from the release of balancing the "I hate myself" statement was so profound for me that I became convinced that this process could help many of my clients. I was right because now many of them come in specifically asking for the muscle-testing and accompanying work.

I encourage you to use the techniques I've described in this chapter. Put it to the test and see if you can rewrite some of what's going on in your own programming. You can't out-perform your self-image. If there are aspects of your self-image that are limiting and holding you back, then focus on those first and rewrite those in your subconscious mind so that you can move more confidently in the direction of your dreams.

You are a work in progress. Whatever has happened in your life up until this moment in time is past. Now it's up to you as to what the future will hold. It is not what happens to you, it is how you respond to what happens to you. Be proactive and take the initiative. Take control of your life. Create the kind of life you want to have. Start on the inside and work your way out.

CHAPTER 22

What You See is What You Get: Being Real

"What other way is there to be?" you might be asking. Unfortunately, the failure to be our authentic self is something we learn early in life. We first get the message from parents that tells us who we are is "not enough." The infant whose instinctive attempts to bond with caregivers that are un-attuned will experience survival terror. Just as with all mammals, there is a biological imperative to attach to the parent for care, feeding, and protection and safety from predators. Her very survival depends on this attachment and when it doesn't happen, she likely forms a core belief that she is unlovable, or defective or maybe even that she's invisible and doesn't really exist. She may also experience the terror that she will die. She then learns to try different behaviors, surrendering her *authentic self* as she seeks attachment. Long before language has been learned, she has practiced the behaviors that work to get her basic physical and emotional needs met. But all at the cost of her authentic self. A little part of her soul has already been lost.

Later, more may be lost as siblings, teachers and even peers fail to "see" her and she goes further underground. The false self is all she knows or remembers, and it gets reinforced as she continues to practice the only way of being in the world that she knows.

To some extent, this little girl is all of us. Everyone is raised by imperfect human beings, and a little part of each one of us is forced underground. As this continues, we may begin the process of attempting to remake ourselves. We see someone else who seems to be more successful than us and so we make up our mind that we're going to be just like them.

That wouldn't be altogether bad if they were a good role model. However, children are all searching to discover who they are and they're in a process of constant development. Therefore, peers do not tend to be the best role models.

We then begin what often becomes a lifelong process of attempting to remake ourselves in the image of what someone else wants us to be. We try to become who or what others expect of us. As I said, this may have started with parents, grandparents or siblings, but as we get older it frequently shows up in the most significant relationship we have as an adult. This seems to be more of a problem for females, although males are not immune (especially if one parent was a narcissist).

In many cultures, females are relationship-oriented and it's generally instilled early-on that they should strive not to be selfish but to find ways to accommodate others first. When this becomes a dominant experience, she may grow up living her life as a "people-pleaser." I don't want you to mistake a giving, caring person who enjoys making others happy and finds satisfaction in that as something negative - that behavior is more like giving a gift. That's not the same as being a people-pleaser. This is someone who seeks to make others happy so that she can feel okay about herself – and this is more about survival.

Whenever we're in survival mode we are not in creative mode. To be a people-pleaser requires constantly reading the landscape to anticipate another person's response, and then constantly adjusting one's own behavior. Assumptions are made based on the perception is of what is being expected of them. In other words, if I'm worried about keeping you happy, then all my energy is going into anticipating how you might respond from one moment to the next. There's no room in there for me to be spontaneous. There's no room for how I may feel about *anything*, because my only concern is worrying about how you may respond to me.

Another hindrance to being authentic is worrying about what you think you *should* be doing, saying, having, or being. This is an internal process that comes from your own programming - through your own culture, the generation you grew up in, the media or your religious background. What you believe about your role is a major influence on your values and behaviors. Although your conscious intellectual mind may argue, you may fear on some deep unconscious level that you are less capable because of your gender, race or religion. Specific messages that were internalized were personalized and became a part of you.

Maybe you aren't as real as you'd like to be because you've spent a lot of your time fantasizing about who you'd like to be and the life you'd like to have. The daydream may have become so fantastic that intuitively you realize this could never come true and that this activity is just an escape from the life you currently know. Since we've talked about visualization and how the dream board plants images in your subconscious mind of the life you'd like to have, how is this different?

It's one thing to imagine yourself the CEO of your own company. It's another to fantasize that you are the monarch of a country. It's fantasy if your daydream involves grandiose images of yourself that have no real connection to your skills, education or even your talents. If you ask yourself what's the likelihood that this could come true for *anyone* (not just for you), the answer should tell you whether it's fantasy or creative visualization.

So then, what is it to be real and authentic? It's empowerment. It's true power - the kind that is associated with truth. After shame, guilt, fear, anger, and pride, finally comes courage. That's empowerment. From this vantage point, we begin to see life as feasible. It is no longer something that has happened to us that has created misery for us or tragedy, nor is it a frightening or antagonistic experience. We have moved into a place of affirmation - of life and of ourselves. We leave behind the lower level emotions. We move into trust, optimism and forgiveness. When we are empowered we are inspiring and hopeful, merciful and accepting. With courage comes exploration, accomplishment and determination. Life becomes an exciting challenge. It's stimulating. You are a producer.

Being inauthentic seems to others as appearing forced. We've all been around the forced smile, or forced friendliness or enthusiasm, and we can feel that something just isn't right. On some instinctual level we know that who they are presenting to us is not who they truly are.

What if you don't like who you are, and you don't think others do either? First off, just know that "What other people think of you is none of your business." So, let go of self-recriminations and harsh self-judgments. They are energy-drainers and will keep you stuck where you are. And now this is where you get down to work. Begin with the internal work - the affirmations; creating a goal statement; meditation, contemplation and prayer; journaling; and visualization, creating a dream board or a dream scrapbook. I recently discovered a powerful online program designed to allow you to create your own personalized ultimate visualization in what is called *Mind Movies*™. Using your own photos, affirmations, and even your favorite song, you can create your own movie. You can transform your visualization board into a digital video vision board. You can learn more about this at www.mindmovies.com.

All of these are designed to recondition your subconscious mind. This is an on-going process throughout your life. You can never afford to allow what life hands you randomly to become your dominant conditioning. Don't allow yourself to go on receiving by default whatever is delivered to you. That's living by default.

Take control of that. There's a constant barrage of messages coming into our subconscious mind from the media, billboards, blogging, conversations overheard in the break room, and the ever-abundant flow of opinions from loved ones. It's a never-ending stream of information and images, most of which are negative. It requires vigilance to protect and maintain that inner environment. Imagine if you'd just washed the floors in your home. You'd take great care to make sure that the dog didn't walk in with muddy paws. In the same way we want to be sure there are no dirty tracks left on our psyche. Your inner environment is even more important than your outer.

The bulk of our attention goes to what's happening externally, when more attention should be paid to what's going on internally. Everything that's external ultimately passes into our internal world. Take control of that - monitor it and make whatever adjustments are necessary. Only expose yourself to environments that will move you in the direction you want to be going. Don't leave it up to chance. If things *just happen* to you, then there's a really good chance that you've not yet exercised control over your experiences.

How would you know if that's happening in your life? One way you'd know is if you've been blaming circumstances or other people for your outcomes. Or if you find yourself feeling powerless over your results. But most importantly, if you feel defeated, deflated, down, negative, confused, lost or hopeless, check your environment.

What about our personal external aspect? What are you projecting that others are seeing? Since we do function to such a great extent using our senses, if *you* are not happy with what you see then change it. One step is to get with an image consultant who can help you with everything from wardrobe, hair, and makeup, to how you carry and present yourself. If you wear the right colors for you and clothes that flatter your unique shape, you're going to feel confident and will attract the right kind of attention.

Do you remember Clark Kent? As Superman, although he possessed superpowers, he still never failed to change into his costume and cape before saving the planet. You also need to have that special outfit that automatically puts you in the mindset of who you want to be projecting. It's a good idea to get a few designer pieces that make you feel put-together when you wear them. This will be your superpower wardrobe.

Maybe you're so unhappy with your body that you don't want to buy new clothes, especially not in a bigger size. We've all been there. If that's the case, then you know it's time to do something about it. There are personal trainers that can coach you to your goal weight and the healthy level of body fat so that you can feel really good in your own skin. They have the training and the expertise to help you establish healthy weight loss goals.

The goal should be fat loss. Weight loss does not always equal fat loss. It's important to learn the difference. You don't want to lose muscle just to see the scale go down. A clean diet and low intensity exercise are two components of a healthy program that will bring your excess body fat down while increasing lean muscle mass. Muscle dictates metabolism. As you increase your muscle mass, your metabolism will rise and you will burn more calories at rest. You can increase your lean muscle mass with weight training.

Incorporating exercise into your life and changing the way that you eat are steps that you'll build up slowly and steadily. Going on a diet is a short-term remedy and rarely has lasting effects. If you look at statistics of all the many weight loss programs, over 90% of dieters regain all the weight and more within two years. I think that's because it's short-term thinking and that always gets short-term results. Instead of focusing on losing weight, it would be better to create a new *lifestyle* in which the goal is to *gain* energy, strength, flexibility, balance and improved health.

Over the course of two years, I experienced some dramatic changes in my own body. In the beginning, I worked out with weights three days per week and steered clear of any aerobics. I felt that what I was doing was enough - because what I was doing before that was nothing! When my trainer moved to another gym where they offered kickboxing, this was something I'd always wanted to do and this allowed me to introduce some aerobic exercise into my routine. As my fitness level improved, my desire for a more sculpted look set in and I became more attentive to what I was eating. Eventually, I added-in classes, which can really be enjoyable alongside like-minded people who encourage and applaud each other's successes.

If my program sounds excessive to you, for me it was the progressive realization of a goal that I'd had for many years – to be as fit as I could be. My mantra became, "If not now, when?" Trust me - it gets easier. As you get results, your motivation increases and so does your enthusiasm.

All of this takes some time. None of us gained weight overnight. It took time to gain the weight and it will take time to lose it, too. That might feel discouraging especially if you have a lot to lose. But like I've told my clients, "You may be discouraged with a three-pound weight loss, but imagine how you'd feel if you had *gained* three pounds." That puts it into perspective, right?

Another aspect to fitness and wellness includes getting sufficient rest and relaxation. There have been numerous studies that have shown a connection between obesity and lack of sleep, and between obesity with cortisol levels and stress, including the stress of *overtraining*. Although working-out is good for you, it's known to create free radical damage. Free radical damage is a natural part of our life processes, but when excessive it leads to inflammation and degenerative conditions. Stressors such as smoking, excessive caffeine consumption, alcohol consumption, medications, pollution, inadequate rest, and overtraining all create excessive free radicals, or oxidation. The oxidation of metal is called rust.

Receiving adequate nutrition is essential to your health and maintaining proper weight. Studies have shown a link between obesity and malnutrition. It is possible for our bodies to take in calories without getting all the nutrients it needs. It is conceivable that the body continues to crave food long after it has consumed more than enough calories, in its attempt to get the vitamins, enzymes and nutrients that it still requires.

This is all a lot of information and you might be feeling a bit overwhelmed. Just know that you only have to start somewhere. It's a cumulative process of learning and forming new habits that create a new lifestyle. In time, you'll surprise yourself with how far you've come without even realizing it, because it's just your new way of living.

Finally, let me offer you this mantra: *I do my best and my best is good enough.* You might be thinking, "… 'good enough'? Is that all?" But think about it … what more could you possibly do than your best? At some point, you must just say, "Enough is enough - what you see is what you get!"

CHAPTER 23

If You Knew You Couldn't Fail... Get the Picture?

What would you do if you knew you couldn't fail? Your life is a mirror image of your current internal reality. We've all lived through our own experiences. Maybe you're currently going through something right now that you feel is unfair or unwarranted by you, but yet here it is smack dab in the middle of your life. You can protest it and cry, "It's not my fault!" Or you can take full responsibility for it and take charge of where things go from here.

Pretend that your life is a movie. Begin to *IMAGE – IN* the life of your dreams. Imagine yourself physically - how you want to look and how that body would feel. Imagine how much money you want in your wallet, in your checking account, your savings and investments. Imagine mentally how would you think, and emotionally how you would feel. What would your relationships look like and feel like? And what would you have in the most important arena - the spiritual arena?

I put that last because we tend to work from the outside in, but really it should be from the inside out because we are *spiritual beings*. This is a good time to take stock. Start a gratitude journal. What do you have now that you didn't have a year ago? Five years ago? Ten years ago? How would you have felt then if you had known what you would have now? As you begin to take stock it will amaze you as you see the many things you take for granted every single day because you are accustomed to having them. They almost fade into the background. Even something as small as a good cup of coffee or tea is something to be grateful for. There are people in this world who can't count on having a fresh drink of water from one day to the next. Those of us in the U.S. throw away more things than many people will ever own in a lifetime. We are truly living in the richest nation on earth and yet often we may feel that something is missing.

To discover what might be missing you will want to get a long-term perspective on your life. Write your own obituary. Imagine that you've passed from this earth and write what those who were closest to you would say about you. Or along the same lines, write a future letter to yourself looking back from the perspective of five years out from this day. This should be future-dated and written in the present tense. It should describe what you've accomplished in each area of your life, as well as what you've learned along the way.

Another mind-expanding exercise is to make a list of a minimum of 100 things you would like to be, do or have. Leave nothing out. Whatever comes to mind add it to the list. Don't prejudge any idea nor try to figure out how you'll make it happen. If it occurs to you, put it on the list. You'll know you're doing it right if your list includes increasingly expansive ideas - things that are over-the-top. Then try to top that. For example, to top your vision of owning a 1,000-acre estate, imagine owning an entire island. If you think it, then it goes on the list. It does not have to be doable from your present perspective.

Now revisit the idea of making a film or a documentary of your life. See yourself in all the exotic places that you've ever felt an attraction to, doing all the things that you've ever thought or dreamed of since you were a child. See yourself being, doing and having these things from your list. Feel what it feels like to be, do and have these things. Pay attention and identify the recurring feelings that you're having. If it is a feeling of freedom, make a mental or written note about that in your journal. If it's about accomplishment or fame, note that. This process can get you in touch with lost feelings - the ones you lost when you lost your ability to dream. It may have been a lifetime ago since you dreamed them, but reconnecting with those feelings now is the key to building a fulfilling life.

If winning an Academy Award is on your list of 100 things you'd like to be, do or have, then connect with the feeling behind that and begin to explore different ways that you can *have that feeling* right now in your life. Feelings are always available. While it might be difficult to see how you'll accomplish winning the Award (and remember that figuring-out the "how" is not part of this exercise), it's highly likely that you can imagine different ways you can have that feeling of fame or recognition. *Ultimately it is just the feeling that we're going after.* People just want to be happy. In the end, how they get there is of little consequence.

A wonderful movie that really exemplifies the feeling of not considering failure while in pursuit of a dream was *August Rush*. I highly recommend this film for its beautiful illustration of the power of belief and faith and in never taking your eyes off your goal. He never falters. Never allow yourself to entertain the idea for one moment that the outcome will be anything other than *that which you desire*. Watch that movie whenever you need to get back in touch with inspiration.

If we can recall how we felt as a very young child anticipating Christmas morning, we'll recall a time of child-like wonder. We didn't worry if Santa had a big enough budget to get us what we so desperately wanted. There was no focus on shortage or lack while we still believed in Santa. Jesus told us to have a child-like faith. That means with full expectation and belief in the delivery of the thing desired. Even those children who grow up in homes where there isn't enough still have child-like faith and hope. It's how we come into the world. It's only through living that we learn to lose it.

It's through focusing on loss or our disappointments in life that cause us to lose hope. We create backup plans – Plan B, we hedge our bets, and we talk about the worst-case scenarios. So much energy goes into focusing on what we don't want. But we've learned that "where our attention goes our energy flows." Rather than creating more of what we don't want, what if we put our attention on those things we *do* want? There is an amazing amount of scripture on the power of believing with faith and holding whatever it is we want in our heart, then speaking only this until we see it come to pass.

The Law of Gender says that there is a time for sowing and reaping. Everything has its period of gestation. We must learn to be patient. It's like digging-up the little seed you planted because it's not sprouting – only to discover that you've just ripped-out the baby roots from the earth. Too often we quit just before what we're waiting for is about to be delivered to us. Try persevering until the end. Refuse to entertain contradictory thoughts. Set your intention to hang-on to your dream and exercise total faith, focusing on what you want, never stopping until you have it in your hand.

Apply this to a goal in your life. Put it to the test. Try holding it in your attention and entertaining no other thought until your goal comes to pass. See what grows while you're waiting. Waiting must be *active* waiting. It must be working toward the thing that you want. This is the action plan that moves you in the direction of your goal. If you identify the thing that you want and then continue to move in that direction, then it cannot fail to be delivered to you.

The only possibility of failure is in quitting. The great philosopher Rumi said, "By passionately believing in that which does not exist you create it. That which is non-existent has not been sufficiently desired."

We are so grounded in our senses and this material world that it's difficult to imagine that it's through our imagination that we create everything that we have. If you just think about it for a moment, you'll realize that everything that you see when you look around you is there because someone had *an idea* to create it - a desk, a cellphone, a laptop, the chair you're sitting in, the computer, and even the tile on your floor. Everything exists because someone first had an idea to create it. Thomas Edison said, "Imagination is the workshop of the mind."

We should cherish our ideas and honor them, rather than dismiss them as inconsequential just because it popped into *our* head. It's important that we recognize that every idea we receive is inspiration. In 1921, Gennevieve Behrand wrote in *Your Invisible Power*:

> Everything has its origin in the mind and that which you seek outwardly you already possess. Your thought of a thing constitutes its origin. Therefore the thought form of the thing is already yours as soon as you think it. Your steady recognition of this thought position causes the thought concentrate to project itself and to assume physical form.

And if you don't believe Gennevieve, in 1937, Napoleon Hill said much the same thing in *Think and Grow Rich*: Whatever the mind can conceive and believe, it can achieve."

CHAPTER 24

You're Either Living or Dying – So GET A LIFE!

A fundamental law of the universe is that nothing stays the same. All of existence is in constant state of change, expanding or contracting, growing or dying. You cannot freeze-frame your life. Nor do we want to when we're faced with difficult times – in those times we're usually quite ready and willing to move on to the next thing in the hope that things will improve.

But when all is well, we don't want change – we want things to stay the way they are. This overlooks one critical truth: when things got good, you noticed it because it was an improvement over the previous condition, which means that change had occurred. The planet has been able to sustain the human race this long because humans have died while new ones were being born. Life brings death and death brings life, and the earth is nourished by the return of its organic elements. Our bodies are comprised of the same mineral compounds that are found in the earth.

Life is a dangerous adventure – no one gets out alive! Most people are hurrying through life trying to make it safely to death. So, while you're alive make the most of it! Start by recognizing yourself first and foremost as a spiritual being. All human beings are spiritual beings before they are anything else. And yet, most people have either lost sight of this or have a hard time accepting it. Notice the term human "being" is not human "doing" despite the fact that we are all racing through life busily engaged in one activity after another. Strive to "be." Connect with the Source of your being-ness. All else will follow naturally.

Many people come to me because they have a sense that there's more to their existence than the life they've been living. They come seeking an experience of their spiritual identity, their soul. Through hypnotherapy, we can do a spiritual regression to a past life and then into their Life Between Lives® where they discover their existence before this life. Here they learn about their purpose and their goals for this life, among many other things. You can read some of Michael Newton's cases in his books *Journey of Souls* and *Destiny of Souls.* Most importantly, the LBL experience offers the *felt sense of being eternal and infinite.* Life is forever changed once that has been directly experienced.

Look inward. Let the locus of control of your life be internal, not external. Right now, put your hand over your heart – feel the beating of it as it pumps the blood to your brain and throughout your body. Recognize right now that you are not responsible for that nor are you even in control of it! You can't stop it and you can't start it. You are dependent for your very life upon something greater than yourself.

You possess a physical body to chauffeur your spiritual being around the physical world you live in. You were given senses to better navigate in your environment, to get your bodily needs met, and to keep you from harm. You were gifted with an intellect which set you above the animals and has endowed your with a higher level functioning – *consciousness.*

Your consciousness is the ultimate gift, in that it allows for self-awareness and the recognition of "I am." It also allows for Self-awareness and the search for a deeper connection with and experience of Spirit. Union with God is the goal of every yogi. The Self is the Divine expression within each one of us. God is omnipresent, therefore you are a temple for His presence. There is no separation between you and God, except for that which your mind/ego perceives. As the servant of the subconscious mind, the ego concerns itself solely with your survival. Its mantra is, "Every man for himself." Consequently, your ego is competitive with others' egos, and is frequently a harsh taskmaster to live with. This creates a sense of individuality, as well as separateness and feelings of loneliness and sometimes isolation.

Your ego wants you to feel different and special, as this reinforces your chances of survival. Realistically, a genuine survival situation would best be served by a spirit of cooperation. However, the ego operates below the level of conscious thinking and functions along the same lines as the animal world, securing the best for itself through primal instincts. Because of the critical functions served by the ego, it tenaciously asserts itself as the authority and purports to know the truth of things. It believes itself to be right and doggedly holds on to its point of view, even to the death of *you*!

The ego is very much like a deity in its own *you-niverse*, but without the benevolence of Spirit, which, on the other hand, is loving, cooperative and creative. Therefore, when you begin to seek out your higher Self and the Spirit within, you are likely to encounter tremendous resistance. Maybe just reading that last line evoked a strong response within you? That would be your ego talking.

Here's the litmus test: if it doesn't feel like love – then it's ego in operation. If it feels loving, cooperative, grateful, generous and creative, then it's Spirit in operation. Abundance will be felt in your core and all good things flow from that.

Your higher Self knows the way home to Spirit. You must take the time to *be*. Prayer, contemplation and meditation are three of the four cornerstones of a life built upon Spirit; love is the fourth. Seek to be a loving person, beginning with yourself. Dedicate your activities to lovingly contributing to others, no matter what the task. Perform your duties as a gift to the universe and to Spirit, even if you're just scrubbing your toilet (...*especially* if!). Be conscious and awake as you go through your day. Look for opportunities to bless others with a smile or a word of encouragement.

Here's one promise I will make: If you approach people and situations with love in your heart and kindness in your actions, you will never feel mistreated again. Although not everyone will return the kindness, you will find that you have acquired understanding and compassion towards all. No one truly wants to be unhappy. Everyone is doing the best they can with what they have to work with in that moment. Do *your* best and do it with *intention*. Take the initiative to set the tone. Do your part in elevating the consciousness on the planet. Take heart in your role as a light to others on their journey. Light your lamp and let it shine.

Hopefully you took the suggestion in the last chapter to create a list of 100 things to be, do and have. If you have not yet begun to create it, begin now. Take that list now and look at it. What happens as you scan the items? Do you feel a jump in your soul as you connect with the ideas you have imaged? This is your Self telling you that those ideas *are relevant to your life. You* thought of them! I know that I personally have not been inspired with the cure for a disease because my talents are not in that area and so I haven't attracted that. However, I do attract people who are struggling with their thoughts and feelings because I can guide them towards healing and wholeness – that's where my heart is.

If it occurs to you to do it, then act on it. Don't delay. Don't entertain doubts – that voice in your head that tells you all the reasons why not to proceed. That's your ego talking, trying to keep you safe … as well as living in a box!

The terror barrier is at the edge of your comfort zone. Imagine how close you are to realizing your dreams when the terror hits – and then push through it! Just on the other side is **freedom from that limiting belief**. Step through into that freedom and experience the release from a self-imposed prison. This is like Plato's story, *Allegory of the Cave,* in which he describes life as an illusion. In the beginning, Plato represents the human condition as prisoners "chained in a cave" with only a fire behind them to light their lives. The people in the cave perceive the world by watching the shadows on the wall. They sit in semi-darkness with only the light of the fire, never realizing that their existence is lacking and knowing nothing else. It's all they've ever known. Plato then tells what happens when some of the prisoners are suddenly released from their chains and let out into the world. A few of them were immediately frightened and wanted to return to the cave and the familiar dark existence! Others looked at the sun and finally saw the world as it really is. A few of them tried to rescue the others.

They would know their previous existence was an illusion, and they would understand that their lives had been one of deception. A few would embrace the sun (the light) and the "real world" and would realize the truth. They would also want to return to the cave to free the others still in bondage. Of course, they would be puzzled by those people still in the cave who would not believe the news of a better reality reported by the "enlightened" truth-bearer. Many would refuse to acknowledge any truth beyond their current existence in the cave. They'd stubbornly remain "in the dark." In fact, some would even attempt to drag the enlightened one back into the darkness, offering reassurances of the safety of the cave.

The prisoners in the cave are the voices of the ego and the paradigms of the subconscious mind, which will try to convince you to stay where you can remain safe and not venture out into "risky" territory.

Now is the time to make a change. Any delay on your part will dilute the power of your intentions and inspiration. Act NOW while you are *feeling* the energy of the idea. Remember, feelings are your experience of the frequency of your vibration. When the feeling is strong, you are magnetically attracting opportunity to yourself. Increase that frequency by giving it your attention, focusing on the potential and enhancing the feelings as you continue to imagine your desired outcome. This should feel like you're having fun. It works every time you work with it – but you must DO SOMETHING! Pablo Picasso once said, "When inspiration comes, *it must find you working.*" (My italics.)

Don't concern yourself with the "how." Just do the very first thing that occurs to you to do. That might be researching some aspect of your idea – google it and get more ideas as you do your research. One idea leads to another. Continuing in this way puts you in action, while you watch the unfolding of the "how."

"Rome wasn't built in a day." Realize that you are setting out on a journey, and plan to enjoy all the sights along the way. It's possible that, halfway through the journey you may alter the itinerary, maybe even change the ultimate destination. That's perfectly fine. If you were bicycling across the U.S. from Los Angeles to New York, and somewhere around Oklahoma City you decided to go to Miami instead, would you feel like a failure and that you were literally *nowhere*? Of course not. You'd be glad that you'd figured that out when you did, *and* you'd recognize that without the original goal of going to New York, you'd still be on the west coast!

Be kind to yourself. Honor the thought that you're always doing the best you can with where you are in this moment of your life. Judgment is always a retrospective demeaning activity – avoid that behavior.

Assess your current outcome and determine if any adjustments are needed and make only those that are necessary. Then stay on your path. Be persistent. Napoleon Hill said, "Persistence creates Faith. And Faith is the only known antidote for failure, it is the starting point of all accumulation of riches, and it is the only agency through which one can tap the force of Infinite Intelligence."

Creativity is forward thinking. Look for ways to be in the creative mode. Live on the edge. Be willing to fail by failing forward. The only true failure is to decide to quit. Everything else is just the operation of the Law of Gender:

Every seed has a gestation or incubation period. Ideas are spiritual seeds and will move into form or physical results. Your goals will manifest when the time is right.

Know that they will and embrace this gift of life that you have been given.

The life you are seeking is, and always has been, seeking you in return.

And the day came when the risk to remain tight in a bud was more painful than the risk it took to blossom.
-Anais Nin

About the Author

Avis Cole Attaway is a licensed Marriage and Family Therapist with a private practice in Riverside, California since 1997, and is currently finishing her Doctorate in Clinical Psychology. Also licensed as a LifeSuccess™ Consultant through Bob Proctor of *The Secret*, Avis works with men and women to transform their lives. As a Spiritual Life Coach who is certified as a hypnotherapist and instructor with The Newton Institute, Avis conducts *Life Between Lives*® spiritual integrations and Past Life Regressions. Trained in shamanic healing practices and Psych-K™ she is also a Reiki Master, and Akashic Records reader.

In addition to a thriving private practice, Avis is also the founder and Director of Life Source Training Institute, a non-profit agency that trains therapists and provides the local community with low cost counseling and family education. Her mission is to reach as many people as possible with healing techniques that are informed by the latest understanding of the brain, mind and body through scientific advances in neurobiology, and integrating this with the recognition of our spiritual essence.

Avis lives with her husband, Bill, and their son, Austin, along with their three dogs and three cats. She enjoys spending time with family and friends, and has a passion for fitness and a love of spiritual studies. Avis is available for speaking engagements and can be contacted at AvisAttawayLMFT@gmail.com.